GLO

Tra

ATHENS

WILLIAM GRAY

NEW HOLLAND

★★★ Highly recommended
★★ Recommended
★ See if you can

First edition published in 2004
by New Holland Publishers (UK) Ltd
London • Cape Town • Sydney • Auckland
10 9 8 7 6 5 4 3 2 1

website: www.newhollandpublishers.com

Garfield House, 86 Edgware Road
London W2 2EA,
United Kingdom

80 McKenzie Street
Cape Town 8001,
South Africa

14 Aquatic Drive,
Frenchs Forest, NSW 2086,
Australia

218 Lake Road,
Northcote, Auckland,
New Zealand

Distributed in the USA by
The Globe Pequot Press, Connecticut

ISBN 1 84330 644 1

Publishing Manager (UK): Simon Pooley
Publishing Manager (SA): Thea Grobbelaar
DTP Cartographic Manager: Genené Hart
Editor: Melany McCallum
Design and DTP: Lellyn Creamer
Cartographer: Marisa Galloway
Picture Researcher: Shavonne Johannes
Consultant: Robin Gauldie

Reproduction by Hirt & Carter (Pty) Ltd, Cape Town
Printed and bound in Hong Kong by Sing Cheong Printing Co. Ltd.

Photographic Credits: Caroline Jones, pages 16, 108; **Chris Hellier**, pages 82, 83, 94, 97; **jonarold.com/J. Arnold**, pages 7, 48, 64, 59, 103, 105; **jonarold.com/W. Bibikow**, page 89; **Neil Setchfield**, pages 4, 12, 17, 23, 27, 29, 30, 36, 37, 40, 41, 45, 49, 50, 65, 66, 67, 68, 69, 100; **Richard Sale**, title page, page 34; **SCPL/Chris North**, pages 13, 14, 35; **SCPL/Elias Rostom**, page 8; **SCPL/Geoffrey Taunton**, page 106; **SCPL/John Howa**, page 96; **SCPL/John Peart,** cover; **SCPL/Patrick Partington**, page 84; **SCPL/Paul Kaye**, page 22; **SCPL/Vangelis Delegos**, page 117; **William Gray**, pages 6, 9, 11, 18, 19, 20, 21, 24, 31, 33, 39, 42, 43, 44, 46, 47, 52, 53, 54, 55, 57, 58, 59, 60, 61, 62, 80, 86, 88, 110, 114, 118; **TI/Nigel Bowen Morris**, pages 28, 38, 63, 91; **TI/Rawdon Wyatt**, page 56; **TI/Simon Reddy**, page 87.
[SCPL: Sylvia Cordaiy Photo Library; TI: Travel Ink]

Keep us Current
Information in travel guides is apt to change, which is why we regularly update our guides. We'd be grateful to receive feedback if you've noted something we should include in our updates. If you have new information, please share it with us by writing to the Publishing Manager, Globetrotter, at the office nearest to you (addresses on this page). The most significant contribution to each new edition will receive a free copy of the updated guide.

Cover: *Crowned by the Parthenon, the Acropolis rises above Athens.*
Title page: *The Tower of the Winds in the Roman Agora, with the Acropolis looming behind.*

CONTENTS

1 Introducing Athens

Think 'Greece' and you may naturally think 'Greek islands'. The capital, Athens, was always going to have a hard time competing with those irresistible specks of holiday heaven scattered throughout the Aegean Sea. And it hasn't helped itself by developing a reputation for congestion and smog. After a day in this vibrant, fascinating city, however, you will soon begin to realize why it is fast becoming a highlight every bit as appealing as Corfu or Lésvos.

Not only is Athens cleaning up its environmental and traffic problems, but it is also polishing its image as one of the world's most important historical cities. To sightsee in Athens is to romp through the ages. From the ancient, yet inspirational, ruins of the **Acropolis** to state-of-the-art developments for the **2004 Olympic Games**, Athens mixes old and new to form an exciting cocktail of architecture, culture and the arts. There are enough ancient monuments, churches and museums to satisfy the most hungry of minds – while great shopping, fine dining and a buzzing nightlife will fulfil those other city-break 'essentials'.

Beyond Athens, in the surrounding region of **Attica**, are more hidden gems, like the Temple of Poseidon at Cape Soúnion or the tranquil monastery of Kaisarianí tucked in woodland on the slopes of Mount Ymittós. Legendary **Delphi** is just a day trip away – as are Epidaurus, Ancient Mycenae and other must-sees of the **Peloponnese**. And, if you still find your mind wandering to those Greek islands, you can always hop on a ferry at the port of **Piraeus** and cruise to the nearby **Saronic Gulf islands**.

Top Attractions

*** **The Acropolis:** crowning glory of Athens, site of the Parthenon and other ancient wonders.
*** **Ancient Agora:** fascinating ruins of Athens' ancient civic centre.
*** **National Archaeological Museum:** treasure house of priceless artefacts.
*** **Delphi:** legendary sanctuary on Mt Parnassós.
** **Cape Soúnion:** setting for the Temple of Poseidon.
** **Hydra:** picturesque Saronic Gulf Island.
** **Argolis:** region of the Peloponnese renowned for ancient sites.

Opposite: *Hadrian's Arch and the Temple of Olympian Zeus.*

Facts and Figures

- Greece occupies an **area** of over 500,000km^2 (193,000 sq miles), of which 131,900km^2 (50,900 sq miles) is land. Greater Athens covers 427km^2 (165 sq miles).
- The highest mountain in Greece is **Mt Olympus** at 2917m (9570ft), while the highest point in Athens is **Lykavitós Hill** at 277m (909ft).
- Greece has a **population** of around 11 million, with an estimated 3.5 million people living in Greater Athens. The next most populous cities are Thessaloníki and Piraeus which have 750,000 and 175,000 inhabitants respectively.

Opposite: *Olive groves and vineyards dominate the cultivated areas of Attica.*
Below: *Philopáppou Hill provides this classic view of the Parthenon with Lykavitós Hill beyond.*

THE LAND

At 277m (909ft) in height, **Lykavitós Hill** is the perfect vantage from which to contemplate the geography of Athens. As you gaze out across the city from the summit of this distinctive, cone-shaped hill, it becomes immediately apparent that Athens lies in a basin surrounded by low ranges to the north, east and west with the sea to the south. You almost get the impression of a concrete reservoir lapping at distant hills, creeping imperceptibly up their slopes and trying to find a gap through which to spread. In fact, that's exactly what this burgeoning city is doing. Greater Athens occupies an area of some 427km^2 (165 sq miles), but every year sees it spilling further into the surrounding region, known as **Attica**. The port of Piraeus on the **Saronic Gulf** has long been assimilated by the Athenian 'urban octopus', as has the northern suburb of Kifissiá.

Shocking as this may sound, the extraordinary and single most redeeming factor about Athens' modern sprawl is the prominence and dignity commanded by one particular hill rising from the city centre. That hill is, of course, the **Acropolis**. By no means the tallest of the city's hills – Lykavitós is 187m (614ft) higher – the Acropolis with its crowning temples retains a sense of serenity and sacredness. There are no city skyscrapers forming a backdrop to the Parthenon – thank Zeus.

The next feature of Athens likely to catch your eye as you survey the scene from any of the city's hills is its close proximity to the **Aegean Sea**. Put in its wider context, Athens lies near the southernmost extremity of the **Balkan Peninsula**. This mountainous land extends from Albania, Macedonia and Bulgaria in the north, and unravels to the south

in a broken mosaic of crenellated coastlines and countless islands in the eastern Mediterranean.

Greece actually has a total of 9841 islands and these, though mostly uninhabited, together with the mainland create a coastline measuring 14,880km (9246 miles). Athens squats on the mainland, but it's only a three-hour drive to the **Peloponnese** – a large peninsula shaped like the leaf of a plane tree that clings to Greece by the **Isthmus of Corinth**. Scattered between the mainland and the Peloponnese are the **Saronic Gulf islands** – close enough to Athens to bring them within easy range of day-trippers.

The Countryside

Find a quiet, undeveloped corner of Attica and you'll no doubt be surrounded by rock-strewn fields and hills, peppered with aromatic herbs and shrubs. In all likelihood, a browsing goat or two will be nearby. This is quintessential Greek countryside – the so-called **maquis** that characterizes much of the Mediterranean region. Another classic piece of the Greek rural jigsaw is the **olive grove** – Greece is the world's biggest producer of this important crop. **Forests**, meanwhile, have largely been cleared for timber and agriculture, but you can still find remnants in the hills where Aleppo pine and Greek fir predominate.

The Coast

Inevitably, the coastline nearest Athens has become heavily developed. South of Piraeus is a string of **beach resorts**, while north and west of the city port is an

Creation Myth

According to Greek mythology the earth goddess, Gaia, was born from a shapeless mass called Chaos. Gaia and her son, Uranus, bore six hideous offspring (three 100-handed giants and three one-eyed Cyclopes) which were cast by their father into the underworld. Gaia then gave birth to seven Titans who avenged their siblings by castrating Uranus. Cronos, leader of the Titans, bore six children with his sister, Rhea. Out of jealousy he swallowed the first five, but Rhea hid the sixth child called Zeus. Later in life, Zeus poisoned his father who promptly regurgitated his remarkably intact brothers and sisters – Demeter, Hades, Hera, Hestia and Poseidon.

industrial amalgam of oil refineries and factories. Roam further along the coast of Attica, however, and you will find quiet secluded coves and fishing villages. A short boat trip from Piraeus will get you to the **islands** of the Saronic Gulf which, although busy at week-ends and during holiday seasons, still provide a taste of the Greek islands – right on the doorstep of Athens.

Climate

Athens has a Mediterranean climate characterized by **hot, dry summers** and **mild winters**. Temperatures peak during July and August when the city can sizzle at over 40°C (104°F). There is little, if any, rain during the summer months – although snow is not unheard of in winter. The mountains of the nearby Peloponnese often receive a heavy snowfall.

ATHENS	J	F	M	A	M	J	J	A	S	O	N	D
MAX TEMP. °C	13	14	16	20	25	30	33	33	29	24	19	15
MIN TEMP. °C	6	7	8	11	16	20	23	23	19	15	12	8
MAX TEMP. °F	55	57	60	68	77	86	92	92	84	75	66	58
MIN TEMP. °F	44	44	46	52	61	68	73	73	67	60	53	47
HOURS OF SUN DAILY	4	5	6	8	9	11	12	12	9	7	5	4
RAINFALL mm	62	37	37	23	23	14	6	7	15	51	56	71
RAINFALL in.	2.4	1.5	1.5	1.0	1.0	0.6	0.2	0.3	0.6	2.0	2.2	2.8
DAYS OF RAINFALL	16	11	11	9	8	4	2	3	4	8	12	15

Flora and Fauna

Wildlife is perhaps not foremost in the minds of many visitors to Athens. Nevertheless, the city does have a few green oases where you can glimpse more than just the ubiquitous street cats and dogs. Some of the best places for city flora and fauna are **archaeological sites**. Kerameikós (*see* page 43), in particular, always has a good show of spring flowers, while butterflies and lizards can also be seen here.

Over 380 species of **birds** can be found in Greece (including one endemic and ten endangered species). Spring and autumn are the best times for bird-watching since these seasons coincide with annual migrations. Although Athens is not one of the country's birding hot spots, it's still worth keeping an eye out for kestrel, short-toed tree creeper, pipits, warblers and flycatchers at the Acropolis, National Gardens and Lykavitós Hill.

However, to better appreciate the variety of flora and fauna in Greece you need to head out of Athens. Mount Párnitha National Park (*see* page 99) and Mount Pendéli, both to the north of the city, support a good range of some of the country's 6000 native wild flower species (including several species of orchids), as well as birds such as redstart, western rock nuthatch and firecrest. Coastal wetlands like the one near Marathon (damaged during construction of the 2004 Olympics rowing venue, but destined to be recreated) provide important habitat for grebes, ducks and other water birds, while a boat trip to any of the islands in the Saronic Gulf will likely be rewarded with a glimpse of **dolphins**.

Wild Flowers

With over 6000 species of wild flowers, Greece has one of Europe's most spectacular floras. There are over 100 types of orchids alone. This diversity is due to the country's variety of habitats (ranging from coastal wetlands to mountains), as well as the fact that much of the land has escaped intensive agriculture. One of the country's best spots for wild flowers is the Peloponnese.

Opposite: *Islands close to Athens, such as Póros, provide an antidote to the hustle and bustle of city life.*

Below: *Parts of Athens, especially protected archaeological sites like Areopagus Hill, are surprisingly green.*

HISTORY IN BRIEF

Dark Ages to Democracy

Athens was inhabited by the end of the **Neolithic Age** (ca.3500BC). Early settlers must have prized the great rock of the Acropolis as an easily defended vantage point – an attribute that holds centre stage throughout the epic, often war-torn, saga of Athens' history.

By 1400BC, the Acropolis had become a **Mycenaean** fortress. Somehow, the citadel survived the

Guide to the Gods

- **Aphrodite** (Venus): goddess of love; mother of **Eros** (Cupid).
- **Apollo**: god of music, poetry and healing.
- **Ares** (Mars): god of war.
- **Artemis** (Diana): Apollo's twin; goddess of hunting.
- **Athena** (Minerva): goddess of wisdom and guardian of Athens.
- **Demeter** (Ceres): goddess of earth and fertility.
- **Dionysos** (Bacchus): god of wine and merriment.
- **Hades** (Pluto): brother of Zeus and god of the Underworld.
- **Hephaestus** (Vulcan): Son of Hera; god of the forge.
- **Hera** (Juno): sister and jealous wife of Zeus.
- **Heracles** (Hercules): god-hero famed for his Twelve Labours (*see* panel, page 12).
- **Hermes** (Mercury): messenger of the gods.
- **Hestia** (Vesta): goddess of the hearth.
- **Poseidon** (Neptune): brother of Zeus and god of the seas.
- **Zeus** (Jupiter to the Romans): the supreme deity; father of the gods.

scourge of the Dorian invasions which coincided with the demise of Mycenae's great empire around 1200BC. The **Dark Ages** that followed, however, were all-consuming. For 400 years, poverty and depopulation racked the region. It was not until 800BC that Athens tentatively emerged as the leader of a group of Attic city-states. A **cultural revival** was underway and, by the 6th century BC, Athens had become the artistic centre of Greece.

The ancient city was haphazardly governed by self-appointed aristocrats who elected the chief priest, general and *archon* (civil ruler). In 594BC, an enlightened archon by the name of **Solon** set in place a radical set of legal, economic and political reforms in an attempt to introduce order to the city. Solon forged the Council of 400, annulled debts and implemented trial by jury. His laws were even put on public display in the Agora. It was nothing short of democracy. A world first.

Conflict with Persia

Unfortunately, a former general, **Psistratos**, could not see the wisdom in Solon's reforms and seized control of Athens in 560BC. Succeeded by his equally tyrannical son, **Hippias**, the dictatorship lasted half a century before the aristocrat **Kleisthenes** sought help from Sparta to overthrow it.

While Hippias scurried off to Persia (whose empire was brooding ominously in the east), Kleisthenes busied himself with new reforms which included dividing Attica into ten tribes, each providing 50 members for the new Council of 500. He also devised ostracism, whereby citizens could vote 'undesirables' into exile for 10 years. Everything seemed to be back to normal until Athens agreed to a request by Ionian Greeks to attack the Persian city of Sardis. Perhaps not surprisingly, Persia responded by landing a large army at **Marathon**. The ensuing battle of 490BC (*see* page 101) amazed everyone by resulting in victory for Athens. Nonetheless, the city's new ruler, **Themistocles**, wisely kept the threat from Persia foremost in his mind. He commissioned a larger navy in the firm belief that it would play a vital

Opposite: *A statue of Athena, the goddess of wisdom and guardian of Athens.*

role in defeating the enemy. He would be proved right. But first it was Persia's turn for some payback.

In 480BC, **Xerxes**, son of the Persian king, Darius, returned to Attica with an invasion force that would have made even the war god, Ares, tremble. Themistocles had little choice but to evacuate Athens which was duly razed to the ground. Fortunes reversed, however, that very same year when Persia's navy was destroyed by Themistocles' fleet at the **Battle of Sálamis** (*see* fact panel on page 112).

Conflict with Persia reached crunch point the following year when Athenians, Spartans and their allies took on the might of the great

HISTORICAL CALENDAR

7000BC Neolithic farmers in northern Greece.
3200BC Bronze Age cultures in Cyclades and Crete.
1400BC The Acropolis becomes a Mycenaean fortress.
1200BC Collapse of Mycenaean empire.
1200–800BC Dark Ages.
490BC Athenians defeat Persians at Battle of Marathon.
480BC Persians destroy Athens.
479BC Athenians, Spartans and allies defeat the Persians at Platéai.
478BC Formation of the Delian League.
461–429BC Golden Age of Pericles; construction of the Acropolis temples.
431–404BC Peloponnesian Wars lead to surrender of Athens to Sparta.
338BC Philip II of Macedon conquers Greek city-states.
336–23BC Alexander the Great extends his empire.
ca.200BC Romans conquer Greece.
AD50 St Paul preaches Christianity in Athens.
124–131 Emperor Hadrian masterminds building programme in Athens.
390 Christianity becomes state religion in Greece.
395 Goths devastate Athens and the Peloponnese; the Roman Empire is divided into Latin west and Byzantine east.
1081–1149 Normans invade Greek islands and mainland.
1456 Ottoman Turks occupy Athens.
1687 Parthenon damaged during Venetian attack on Turkish magazine.
1814 Foundation of Filikí Etaireía, Greek liberation movement.
1821 Greek flag of independence raised on 25 March.
1827 Battle of Navaríno.
1828 Ioannis Kapodistrias becomes first president of Greece.
1831 President Kapodistrias assassinated.
1832–62 King Otto rules.
1834 Athens replaces Nafplio as capital.
1864 Greece becomes crown democracy; Greek Orthodoxy made state religion.
1920–23 Following WWI, Greece continues a war against Turkey ending in defeat.
1923 Population exchange with Turkey.
1941 Italian and German invasions lead to serious food shortages in Athens where some 40,000 people perish.
1951 Greece joins NATO.
1967 Military junta siezes power.
1974 Junta is overthrown.
1975 New republican constitution put in place.
1981 Greece joins the European Community.
1985 Athens becomes Europe's first Cultural Capital.
2002 Euro replaces the drachma as Greece's currency.
2004 Athens hosts the 2004 Olympic Games.

eastern empire at **Plataea** (near Thebes). By all accounts it was a gruelling, bloody battle between equally matched armies of 100,000 soldiers. The Persian forces were defeated – an event recorded by Herodotus as the 'finest victory of all history'.

The Golden Age

Themistocles, forever a visionary, wasted little time in commissioning new warships and defensive walls around Athens. He also set in place the **Delian League**, an alliance of 200 city-states (though *not* including old rivals, Sparta) that swelled Athens' army, navy and treasury in return for protection from the Persians.

In 461BC, the treasury was moved from Delos Island to Athens. Flush with cash, **Pericles** (who ruled Athens from 461–429BC) launched his spectacular building programme, culminating in such marvels as the Acropolis temples (*see* pages 30–37). Athens embraced its Golden Age in a proactive flurry of science, art and culture. Big names riding this wave of inspiration and achievement included **Pheidias**, the master sculptor, **Herodotus** the historian, **Socrates** the philosopher and playwrights like **Aristophanes**, **Sophocles** and **Euripides**. In the 5th century BC, the basis of western culture was being forged in Athens. It was *the* place to be. Neighbouring Sparta was turning green with envy. Conflict was inevitable.

In 446BC, the two powers signed a peace treaty, but it wasn't worth the stone it was etched in. The **Peloponnesian Wars** (dragging on from 431–404BC) began with Sparta taking Attica. Pericles had planned for the likely danger of a siege and had strengthened the city walls down to Piraeus – but he couldn't have foreseen the plague that later decimated the city's population and claimed his own life. Athens finally toppled following

LABOURS OF HERACLES

Greatest of the Greek heroes, **Heracles** was immortalized by successfully completing the seemingly impossible 'Twelve Labours' set by Eurystheus, King of Mycenae. The first two tasks involved slaying the Nemean lion and the many-headed Lernaean hydra. For his Sixth Labour, Heracles had to kill the man-eating Stymfalian birds, while the Eighth Labour demanded the capture of the horses of Diomedes which, perhaps not surprisingly, were also fond of human flesh.

the naval defeat at Aegospotami. Sparta tore down the city walls, abolished the Delian League and introduced a brutal new regime. In 399BC, Socrates was executed for allegedly corrupting the youth with his speeches. By 378BC, a public revolt had expelled the occupiers and Athens had set up a second Delian League – but the city was a shadow of its former self. And there was more unrest on the horizon.

Pericles (ca.495–429BC)

Background: Athenian statesman, orator and military leader elected to high office (*archon*) every year from 443BC to his death.
Achievements: strengthening the Greek navy and Athens' leadership of the Delian League, as well as developing Athens as a great cultural centre.
Best known for: masterminding the building programme in Athens (including the Parthenon on the Acropolis) which became known as the Golden Age of Pericles.

Macedonians, Romans and Christianity

In 338BC, **Philip II of Macedonia** defeated the Greeks at the Battle of Chaironeia and took control of the city-states. Two years later, following Philip's assassination, his son, **Alexander the Great**, became king and the centre of Greek culture shifted from Athens to Alexandria, Rhodes and Pergamon. When Alexander died in Babylon in 323BC, Athens was left to be squabbled over by a succession of his generals.

The **Roman** army moved in decisively in 197BC, squashing the Macedonians and 'liberating' Greece – of most of its art and sculpture, if nothing else. While booty was being hauled back to Rome, the new invaders sacked Corinth (146BC) and laid waste to the Ancient Agora and walls of Athens (86BC). In many respects, though, the Romans were highly cultured and soon began endowing Athens (and other sites) with many fine monuments – particularly under the reign of **Emperor Hadrian**. The city once more became a major seat of intellect, while **Pausanias**' *Guide to Greece* (produced in AD170) proved invaluable for the new breed of Roman tourists 'doing the sights'.

By now, Christianity was well afoot. **St Paul** had first preached in Athens around AD50. By AD390, pagan Greek and

Opposite: *Apollo stands supreme atop an Ionic column at the Athens Academy.*
Below: *A small church at the harbour of Aegina, one of the Saronic Gulf Islands.*

Lord Byron (1788–1824)

Background: British poet.
Achievements: publication of *The Maid of Athens* and parts of *Childe Harold*, inspired by his visits to Athens.
Best known for: his poetry and as a high-profile campaigner for Greek Independence.

Roman gods had been banned, followed three years later by cult festivals like the Olympic Games. Christianity was established as the state religion in Greece.

Not that all the world was at peace. Far from it. **Goths** had been flexing their barbarian muscles in the north since AD252 and, in 395, they swept through Athens and devastated the place. Emperor Theodosius I died the same year and the Roman Empire was divided into Latin west and Byzantine east.

Christianity continued to spread during the Byzantine era. In AD529, **Emperor Justinian** ordered the replacement of classical schools of philosophy with Christian theology ones. The Parthenon became a cathedral. Generally, though, it was a rough time for Athenians. Barbarians periodically invaded; there were earthquakes and, to top it all, another plague. Then, in 1081, **Normans** stormed in, signalling the start of a series of invasions by Franks, Florentines and Venetians.

Below: *Even in ruins, the approach to the summit of the Acropolis is magnificent.*

The Ottoman Occupation

In 1456, **Turks** invaded Athens, beginning nearly 400 years of Ottoman occupation that would witness the Parthenon's role changing once again – this time to a mosque. **Venetians** tried on several occasions to seize the city. Morosini's infamous bombardment in 1687 literally raised the roof of the Parthenon – though, admittedly, the Turks were using it as a powder magazine at the time. In 1801, the British Ambassador in Constantinople, **Lord Elgin**, helped himself to the best bits of the ruined temple's frieze and sold them to the British Museum in London. The battle to have the so-called Elgin Marbles (*see* fact panel on page 32) returned to their homeland has become a long one. In contrast, Turkish occupation was contested and decisively resolved during the **War of Independence**.

Above: *Symbolizing the struggle for independence, the blue and white Greek flag was first raised on 25 March 1821.*

Greek Rebellion to European Union

The secret Greek liberation movement, **Filikí Etaireía**, signalled the war's commencement by raising the rebel flag on 25 March 1821. The 1827 **Battle of Navaríno** ended the war when the Turks lost 6000 men and 53 ships in the momentous naval scrap in the southwest Peloponnese.

The following year, **Ioannis Kapodistrias** became the first president of Greece, but when he was assassinated in 1831, Britain, France and Russia stepped in to establish a new monarchy under the reign of **King Otto** of Bavaria. Otto, facing the huge task of regenerating a war-torn and depopulated Athens, initiated an ambitious neoclassical building boom. But in 1862, **Revolution** drove the king from Greece. Two years later, a new constitution declared Greece a 'crown democracy' and Greek Orthodoxy was made the state religion. In 1893 the Corinth Canal was opened, while 1896 heralded the revival of the Olympic Games.

For several years, a steady stream of country folk had been moving to the city in search of work, but in 1923 the floodgates opened. Greece had made a failed attempt to seize former territory from Turkey and the resultant **Treaty of Lausanne** involved the expulsion of over a million Greeks – most of whom returned to Athens. The explosion of poorly planned, cheap construction – the start of the city's urban sprawl – dates from this time.

World War II struck another blow to Athenians – more died from starvation than anything else during German occupation. Unrest perpetuated a bitter civil

Melina Mercouri (1922–1994)

Background: actor turned politician.
Achievements: starring in films, such as *Never on Sunday* and *Topkapi*, and becoming the Minister of Culture in 1981.
Best known for: Pioneering the concept of the European City of Culture and campaigning for the return to Athens of the Elgin Marbles.

Above: *Contemplating life, a trio of local men relax on the island of Spétses.*
Opposite: *Greece is almost entirely Greek Orthodox in religion.*

war that lasted until 1949. Many Greeks migrated to the United States, Canada and Australia. In 1967, right-wing army colonels (the Junta) launched a **military coup** which reached its darkest moment on 17 November 1973 when tanks stormed a protest at Athens' Polytechnic, killing 20 students. The Junta was overthrown the following year; a referendum abolished the monarchy (which remains in exile) and the socialist PASOK government of **Andréas Papandréou** was elected in 1981. In the same year Greece joined the **European Community** (EC).

Olympic Fortunes

By the end of the 1980s, Athens had a reputation as one of Europe's most polluted and traffic-congested cities. But the following decade witnessed a turning point. In 1989, the New Democracy (the main right-wing political party) was voted into power with **Konstantinos Karamanlis** becoming president (he was succeeded in 1998 by **Kostis Stefanopoulos**). In 1993, Andréas Papandréou won a third term in government – followed by **Kóstas Simítis** in 1996. But perhaps more important than these political changes was the positive mood that swept Athens in 1997 following the decision to award the city the **2004 Olympic Games**. A new-found confidence (and billions of euros of investment) have urged the capital to get its act together. A new international airport has been built; museums and monuments are being renovated, while traffic and pollution problems are being tackled head-on with new metro and tram systems, pedestrianization and tree planting. It may not necessarily herald another 'golden age' for Athens, but it will certainly add to the pleasure and excitement of visiting (or living in) this dynamic city.

2004 Olympics Mascots

Wearing the colours of the Greek sea and sun, *Athena* and *Pheros*, the mascots for the 2004 Olympic Games in Athens, were inspired by a bell-shaped, terracotta Greek doll dating from the 7th century BC. Known as a *daidala*, the ancient artefact is held in the city's National Archaeological Museum.

GOVERNMENT AND ECONOMY

Greece has been a parliamentary republic with a president as head of state since 1975. The president and 300-member parliament have joint legislative power. Athens, which is part of the prefecture of Attica, entered the European Monetary Union in January 2002 when the drachma was phased out to make way for the euro (¤). The country's economy has been improved through structural reform and a comprehensive programme of deregulation and privatization of the telecommunication, electricity, shipping and airline industries. Greece has the third highest Gross Domestic Product (GDP) growth rate in the European Union. Tourism is one of the biggest earners (with over 12 million tourist arrivals a year), while the majority of the workforce is employed in either services or industry. The average wage is approximately ¤13,000 per annum. Unemployment remains stubbornly high at around 11%, although inflation dropped from 20% in 1990 to 3.6% in late 2001.

GREEK ORTHODOX EASTER

Easter is the most important religious event in the Greek Orthodox calendar. At dusk on Good Friday, a bier decorated with flowers and containing an effigy of Christ is carried through the streets. Church services are held at midnight on Easter Saturday, followed by candle-lit processions, celebrations and feasting on Easter Sunday – traditionally a time for families to reunite.

THE PEOPLE

Of a total population of 3.5 million, some 600,000 Athenians are immigrants – a number that continues to grow with new arrivals from Albania, the Balkans, the former Soviet Union and other parts of the world. Many Athenians are descended from families evicted from southwest Turkey during the 'population exchange' of 1923.

Religion

About 98% of the Greek population belong to the Greek Orthodox Church with the remainder being mostly Roman Catholic, Jewish or Muslim. Several religious festivals dominate the Greek year, the most important being

Olympics 2004 Developments

Athens' successful bid for the 2004 Olympics led to a welcome injection of investment in and around the capital. In addition to the opening of Elefthérios Venizélos International Airport in 2001, developments have included 120km (75 miles) of new highways, extended suburban and light rail links, a 24km (15-mile) tram network, Europe's most modern metro system, new sports and recreational complexes, landscaped pedestrian walkways unifying Athens' archaeological and major cultural sights, a Green Spaces programme, waste management and recycling initiatives, and the introduction of environmentally friendly transportation vehicles.

Easter. In Greek culture, 'name days' (celebrating the saint after whom a person is named) are more important than birthdays. Also of great significance are weddings and funerals. Greeks are generally quite superstitious and believe in the 'evil eye' (bad luck brought on by envy) so take care not to be too effusive when complimenting things of beauty – especially newborn babies.

Sport and Recreation

Since ancient times, Greeks have been more than a little keen on sport – something that is set to receive a huge boost in the wake of the **2004 Olympic Games**. The country's most popular sport is **soccer** – the top three teams are Panathinaikos, AEK and Olympiakos. **Basketball** and **horse racing** also have a dedicated following.

In Athens, residents and visitors can enjoy a number of recreational activities. **Jogging** is popular around the maze of paths in the National Gardens, around Kallimármaro Stadium and, if you feel like a challenge, up Lykavitós Hill. **Swimming** is limited to hotel pools and the public pool opposite the Zappeion (otherwise head to the coastal resorts between Piraeus and Vouliagméni and the islands of the Saronic Gulf). There is an 18-hole **golf** course at Glyfáda and **sailing** marinas in Piraeus and various coastal resorts.

The Olympic Games

The first Olympic Games were held every four years (or *olympiad*) at Ancient Olympia (*see* page 119) from as early as 776BC. Dedicated to the gods, they originally had a religious focus with many of the sporting events based on ancient Greek myths. Men from all corners of the ancient Greek world came to compete. Victory was rewarded with an olive wreath – not to mention considerable prestige and power. Dismissed as a pagan cult, the games were banned in 393AD by Emperor Theodosius and were not reinstated until 1896 when the first modern Olympic Games were held in Athens.

In 2004, the city once again hosts the premier sporting event that has come to embody world peace through the Olympic Truce. Taking place from 13–29 August 2004, the competition schedule includes 28 Olympic sports held at 37 venues.

Above: *Contemporary Byzantine-style icon paintings for sale in Pláka.*
Opposite: *An impressive feature of Ancient Olympia in the Peloponnese, the* palaestra *was a training centre for boxers, wrestlers and jumpers.*

History of Art and Architecture

Ancient Greeks endowed the world with art and architecture that not only takes pride of place in many of today's great museums, but also influenced several great creative minds and movements – from Picasso to the Italian Renaissance.

Cave paintings, clay fertility figures, Minoan pottery and the haunting, severe figurines from the Cycladic Islands mark the emergence of Greek art in the **Neolithic and Early Helladic** period from 5000–2000BC (see fact panel on page 66). The following four centuries of the **Middle Helladic** period witness more advanced Minoan frescoes and ceramics, while the **Late Helladic** period (1600–1100BC) is marked by the great Mycenaean citadels with their cyclopean walls, elaborate gateways, gold burial treasures and impressive *tholos* tombs like the Treasury of Atreus at Mycenae.

The Dark Ages (or **Geometric** period) from 1100–770BC are characterized by pots with simple dark bands (the so-called granary style) – but little else. Artistic juices begin flowing again during the **Archaic** period

ATHENS CENTRAL MARKET

Located on Athinias and Evripidae streets (open early until late, Monday–Saturday), the Central Market is a fascinating place to wander around – even if you're not interested in buying any of the vast range of meat and seafood on sale. On nearby streets you will find stalls piled high with a variety of nuts, spices, olives, fruits, vegetables and cheeses.

(770–500BC) with Corinthians pioneering black-figure vase painting around 700BC. Red-figure vases depicting mythological scenes appear in Athens ca.530BC, while formal, Egyptian-like statues (male *kouros* and female *kores*) begin to appear in cult sanctuaries. The first wooden peristyle temples (columns on all sides) date from 718BC, while the oldest Doric temple still standing is the Temple of Apollo (550BC) in Ancient Corinth.

Calendar of Events

- **6 January – Epiphany:** Blessing of the waters at Piraeus where men dive into the sea to retrieve a cross.
- **February – Carnival:** Music, dance and fancy-dress parades in Pláka.
- **February/March – Ash Monday:** Kites are flown from city hills.
- **25 March – Independence Day:** Military or school parade celebrating the Greek uprising against Turkish occupation.
- **1 May – Labour Day:** Workers' parades.
- **Summer – Athens Festival and Epidaurus Festival:** Music, drama and dance at historical theatres in Athens and the Peloponnese.
- **July – Rockwave:** Three-day rock music festival.
- **28 October – Óchi Day:** Military parade in honour of General Metaxas who rejected Mussolini's request for Italian troops to use Greek ports with a terse '*Óchi*' ('No').

The **Classical** period (500–323BC) sees Greece oozing confidence after its victory over Persia. Ambitious and innovative designs – reaching their climax with the Parthenon – are indicative of the general mood. Temples are more than just imposing structures – they are works of art with remarkable friezes and sculptures depicting gods, mythological battles and great festivals, such as the Panathenaic Procession. Classical statues, like the bronze of *Poseidon* (*see* page 67), are more lifelike, while the cities themselves flourish with elaborately planned agoras, gateways and walls.

While Pheidias dominated the classical period of sculpture, the **Hellenistic** period (323–30BC) has another master sculptor – Praxiteles of Athens – renowned for his graceful statues of figures, such as *Hermes* (*see* page 120). The **Roman** period (30BC–AD330) is distinguished by another building boom with Athenian landmarks like Hadrian's Arch and the Theatre of Herodes Atticus being constructed.

During **Byzantine** times (AD330–1452) the first churches designed to the Greek cross plan are built. Following **Iconoclasm** (AD723–843), when figurative art was equated with idolatry and destroyed, came new monasteries adorned with dazzling mosaics of holy scenes.

Only a few mosques (such as Fethiye Djami Mosque in the Roman Agora) remain in Athens from the period of **Turkish** occupation (1460–1830). **Post-Independence** sees cities being rebuilt – first with neoclassical buildings, such as the Academy in Athens (designed by prominent architects like Ernst Ziller), then by modern urban sprawl during the 1950–1970s and, most recently, by efforts to restore the gems of ages past.

WHAT TO BUY

Food and drink: olive oil, honey, ouzo, retsina. **Souvenirs:** worry beads, copper coffee pots, icon paintings, museum replicas. **Goods:** ceramics, rugs, leather, gold jewellery.

The Arts

Athens has a lively **drama** scene dating from the 6th century BC when the Dionysia Festival (*see* panel on page 42) took place. Today, the works of great playwrights such as Aeschylus, Aristophanes, Euripides and Sophocles are still performed in the capital – along with contemporary ballet and theatre.

Music also runs in the Greek blood. Everything from folk to rock can be sampled at various venues during summer. Rembetika – a kind of Greek Blues – is a hybrid of traditional Greek music and mellow overtones introduced by homesick immigrants from Asia Minor. An evening at one of Athens' Rembetika bars can be highly atmospheric.

On the **literature** front, celebrated ancient poets like Alcaeus, Pindar and Sappho have contemporary counterparts in the form of Constantine Cavafy and two Nobel Prize laureates, George Seferis and Odysseus Elytis. Nikos Kazantzakis, author of *Zorba* and *The Last Temptation*, remains the most renowned 20th-century Greek novelist.

With numerous galleries opening across the capital (particularly in the districts of Psirrí and Omónia), Athens' **contemporary arts** scene is flourishing. Try Zoumboulakis Gallery in Syntagma for contemporary posters and prints.

Opposite: *Black-figure vases cram the shelves of a curio shop in Monastiráki.*
Below: *Elegant 18th-century mansions surround Hydra's harbour.*

Temple Terminology

Capital: top of a column, either simply or elaborately carved, depending on the temple's architectural order (Doric, Ionic or Corinthian).
Caryatids: statues of women used instead of columns.
Cella: innermost room or sanctuary.
Entablature: everything above the column capitals.
Metopes: sculptured panels on a frieze.
Pediment: triangular part crowning ends of temple.

Five Great Temples

1. The Parthenon, Acropolis
2. Temple of Olympian Zeus, Athens
3. Temple of Poseidon, Cape Soúnion
4. The Erechtheion, Acropolis
5. Temple of Aphaia, Aegina

Architecture

Athens boasts an extraordinary range of architectural styles, from 5th century BC cult temples to 21st century AD sports complexes and state-of-the-art museums. Architecture is the capital's hallmark – a head-spinning kaleidoscope of weathered Roman columns, stylish neoclassical mansions, austere office blocks and slick marble-and-glass metro stations.

Temples are characterized by Doric, Ionic and Corinthian columns – the latter being the most elaborate with their leafy scrolls. Byzantine **churches** are scattered throughout the capital, tucked away like terracotta nodules in a modern conglomerate of shops and restaurants. Typically, they feature a central dome flanked by vaults with smaller domes at the corners and three apses to the east.

Food and Drink

Eating out is a highlight of any visit to Athens. In addition to well-known favourites like Greek salad, moussaka and gyros, there is a mouth-watering range of dishes based on local and international cuisine (from sushi to spaghetti). At one extreme, you can dine like an ancient Greek at *Archaion Gefsis* (in Piraeus) which serves huge portions of roast meats and fish – and at the other, you can pop into *McDonalds* (Syntagma Square) for a takeaway burger and fries.

A traditional Greek meal starts with bread and a selection of starters (***mezédes***). These can include anything from *tzatziki* (cucumber, yoghurt and garlic dip) and *saganáki* (fried cheese) to meatballs and prawns. Sweet Florina peppers, pistachio nuts and, of course, olives also make tasty pre-dinner nibbles.

Main dishes range from herb-rich rural stews like *stifádo* (beef with potatoes and onions) and *arní me vótana* (lamb on the bone with beans and potatoes) to delicious seafood, such as *kalamária* (squid) and prawns.

Below: *Tasty trio:* soutzoukákia *(herb-flavoured meat balls) with fried aubergines and tomato salad.*

Left: *Traditional Greek coffee is brewed in a long-handled* mpriki *using very finely ground beans.*

It's worth bearing in mind that many places start cooking around mid-morning and keep dishes warm until lunch. If you want food piping hot choose something that needs to be freshly cooked liked *souvláki* (meat or fish kebabs) or grilled fish. Remember, too, that Greeks generally eat much later than you may be used to.

Desserts are not often eaten during a main meal. Cakes, puddings and ice cream are usually enjoyed as afternoon snacks after a long siesta. Sweets include *loukoumia* (yeast donuts in syrup) and *chalvas* (sweetmeats).

If eating 'on the hoof' between a hectic round of sightseeing is called for, then Athens' numerous street vendors can oblige with tasty **street snacks** like *koulouri* (sesame seed bread rings), *tyropitta* (cheese pies) and *bougátsa* (custard tarts).

Depending on what and where they are eating, Greeks may drink beer, water, wine, retsina, ouzo or softdrinks with their meals. The local **wine** industry has begun developing a good reputation and you should look out for leading brands, such as Boutari, Domaine Carras and Kourtakis. By contrast, the famous **retsina** (resinated white wine) will always be an acquired taste – as will the aniseed-flavoured Greek aperitif, **ouzo**. Popular with the younger 'in crowd', ***frappé*** is basically iced instant coffee – pale and frothy compared to traditional strong **Greek coffee** drunk in a tiny cup and served from a long-handled *mpriki* coffee pot.

Where to Eat

Tavernas are casual, often family-run, restaurants offering traditional and good-value food and house wines. ***Estiatórias*** are more sophisticated restaurants with a wider range of dishes and wines, while ***psistarias*** specialize in grills and spit roasts and ***psarotavernas*** focus on seafood. A ***medezopolis*** offers a range of small meze dishes which, at an ***ouzeri***, are washed down with glasses of ouzo.

All about Olives

Ancient Greeks believed the olive tree was a gift from the gods. Not only did they start clearing the country's native forest to grow olive plantations, but in the 6th century BC Solon introduced a death sentence to anyone convicted of cutting down one of the sacred trees. Today, there are some 130 million cultivated olive trees in Greece, producing the world's greatest variety of olives – from fat, juicy Ionian green olives to sweet, dark Kalamátas varieties. Following harvest, olives are either pressed to make oil or preserved in brine, oil, salt or water.

2
Athens

Home to nearly four million people, Athens is undergoing a long-awaited renaissance. Pedestrianized areas are beginning to link the capital's ancient monuments, museums and shopping streets. There is a new international airport. Metro and tramlines are removing the sting from the city's once-notorious traffic and pollution problems. Tree-planting, hotel refurbishment… the list goes on.

Pericles, the city's ruler during its golden age in the 5th century BC, would have been pleased to see this latest phase of regeneration. He, too, was a visionary. Many of Athens' most celebrated monuments, including the **Acropolis** temples, were down to him. Reigning supreme over the city almost two and a half thousand years after their creation, the **Parthenon**, **Propylaia** and **Erechtheion** form a sacred trio no visitor should miss. Beneath the Acropolis are the less imposing, but equally fascinating ruins of the **Ancient Agora** – birthplace of western democracy and a truly enlightening glimpse into the lives of ancient Greeks.

Ancient **theatres** can be found on the southern side of the Acropolis, while to the north, in **Pláka** and **Monastiráki**, you will come across many other historical nuggets – from Roman remains to Byzantine churches. Further afield, **Syntagma Square** forms the lively hub of the city – radiating routes north and east to fine museums, including the **National Archaeological Museum**, home to such treasures as Mycenaean gold and Hellenistic bronze statues.

Don't Miss

*** **The Acropolis:** iconic city centrepiece – the Parthenon, Propylaia and Erechtheion are unmissable.
*** **Ancient Agora:** interesting ruins and museum evoking life in ancient Athens.
*** **National Archaeological Museum:** the Mycenaean gold and Hellenistic bronzes are star exhibits.
*** **Pláka and Monastiráki:** historic streets riddled with churches, Roman ruins, tavernas, markets and shops.
** **Syntagma Square:** bustling hub of the modern city, famous for evzone guards.

Opposite: *The remaining Corinthian columns of the Temple of Olympian Zeus.*

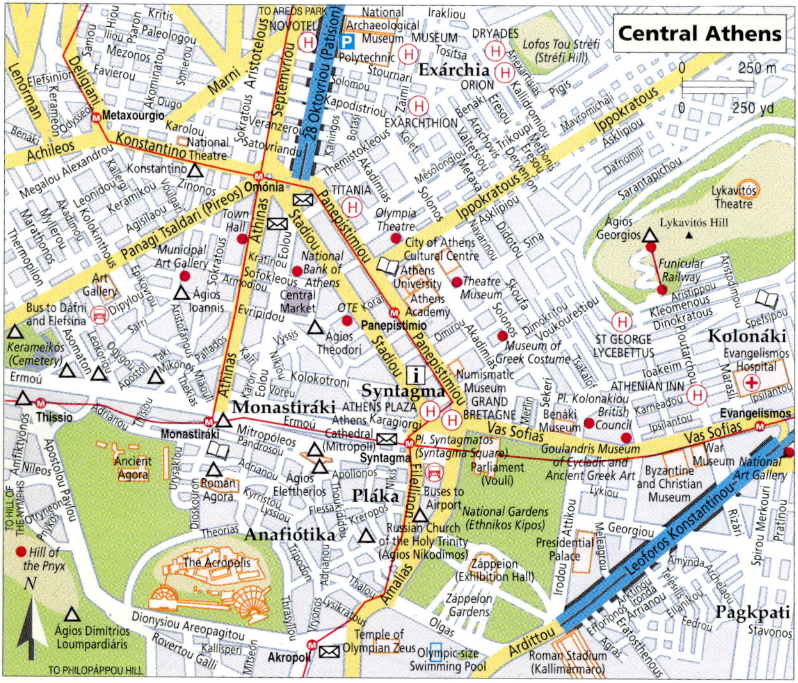

Athens is a walker's city. Its main sites are concentrated near the centre and, on foot, you will get to meet its people – from street vendors selling bread rings to market traders hawking old coins. See the sites, peruse the museums and shop for curios – but, above all, take your time. No visit to Athens would be complete without an hour or two daydreaming at the top of **Lykavitós Hill** or a long, lazy lunch at a taverna.

Athens by Area

The **Acropolis** has always been the focus of life in Athens, so it's not surprising that most of the city's major landmarks and attractions are found on and around this rocky outcrop. As well as the Parthenon and other famous temples on top, the Acropolis has two ancient drama **theatres** hewn from its southern slope. A compact cluster of **hills** to the west provides superb views of the Acropolis, as well as the remains of the **Ancient Agora** that spreads beneath its northeast flank.

Immediately to the north of the Acropolis are the historic districts of **Pláka** and **Monastiráki**, boasting plenty of fine monuments, museums and churches (including the Roman Agora and Athens Cathedral), not to mention some of the city's most enticing shopping and dining.

Moving eastwards, **Syntagma** is the city centre of modern Athens with its bustling square, classical buildings and historic **National Gardens**. Major roads lead north and east from here.

The easterly route will take you into **Kolonáki**, home to some outstanding museums as well as fashionable (and expensive) shops and restaurants. Kolonáki also provides access to **Lykavitós Hill** – another prominent city landmark offering wonderful views.

Head north from Syntagma and you will experience modern Athens blended with neoclassical gems (such as the Academy) before reaching **Exárchia** and the world-renowned **National Archaeological Museum**. Further afield is the leafy, upmarket suburb of **Kifissiá**. This is best reached by metro – as is **Irini**, the site of the 2004 Olympic Stadium.

ABBREVIATIONS

EHS urban railway service
ELPA Touring and Automobile Club of Greece
ELTA the post office
EOT tourist information office
KTEL private bus service
OASA/ETHEL public bus service
OSE the railway organization
OTE the telephone service

Sightseeing in Athens

The best way to take in the major sites of Athens is on foot. Not only are many of the star attractions concentrated in a relatively compact area, but they are also being linked by an ambitious €4.4 million pedestrianization project.

The over riding factor to take into account before you hit the sightseeing trail is the time of day. Summer in Athens can be oppressively hot, so it's best to visit archaeological sites first thing in the

Below: *Athens is home to some 3.5 million people.*

Street Snacks

Wherever you're walking in Athens there's usually a street food stall nearby. Sesame bread rings are a popular snack, as are roasted chestnuts and honey cakes. For something more substantial, head to the Mitropóleos area of Monastiráki where you will find a mouth-watering array of *souvláki* – meat, fish or vegetables grilled on a skewer and served in a pitta bread.

morning before retreating to a museum when temperatures start to soar. Early birds will also catch the best light for photography and miss the large tour groups. Another reason to go sooner rather than later is that many sites and state-run museums close early afternoon.

Sightseeing essentials include comfortable shoes with good grips (ancient marble surfaces tend to be slippery and riddled with potential ankle-twisters), sun hat and sunscreen, camera and plenty of film (although many museums prohibit interior photography or the use of a flash or tripod).

Don't worry about the possibility of getting lost in Athens. As long as you don't stray too far off the beaten track you should always be able to get a bearing on the Acropolis, or distinctively shaped Lykavitós Hill. Many Athenians speak some English and will usually be only too happy to point you back in the right direction.

Of more potential concern to the visitor is the stress of coping with the city's traffic, noise and pollution. The trick here is to plan a modest bout of sightseeing each day, with 'quiet time' allocated in the parks and gardens or at a taverna, and to intersperse city days with excursions further afield. The metro, for example, can whisk you to Piraeus where ferries depart for the Saronic islands, while organized coach tours regularly ply routes to Cape Soúnion, Delphi and the Peloponnese.

Below: *The museum at Gytheion is just one of the sights to explore while visiting the Peloponnese.*

Suggested Itineraries

One day

With limited time, your main priorities have to be the Acropolis and National Archaeological Museum. Intersperse these with a leisurely meal at a taverna in Pláka, a browse through the Monastiráki flea market and a quick stop at the Parliament to watch the changing of the guards.

Two days

Stroll the Ancient and Roman Agoras, visit the Tower of the Winds and have coffee in the square beneath the Mitrópoli (Cathedral). Delve into the treasures of the Benáki Museum and enjoy lunch in the museum's restaurant overlooking the National Gardens. Visit the Museum of Cycladic Art and the Byzantine and Christian Museum. Go window-shopping in Kolonáki before taking the funicular railway up Lykavitós Hill to watch nightfall over Athens.

Above: *The metro provides a fast and reliable means of transport in Athens.*

Three days

Spend a quiet couple of hours in the ancient and atmospheric cemetery of Kerameikós before walking to the ancient theatres of the Acropolis and on towards the Temple of Olympian Zeus and the old Olympic Stadium (Kallimármaro). Spend the afternoon on a tour (or drive yourself) to Cape Soúnion to watch the sunset at the Temple of Poseidon.

Five days

Spend a morning at Moní Kaisarianí nestled in pine forest on the slopes of Mount Ymittós, followed by an afternoon exploring the maze of streets in Pláka's Anafiótika quarter and shopping for souvenirs. On the next day hire a car or join an organized tour to the Peloponnese, visiting the canal and ancient remains at Corinth, the historic coastal city of Nafplio and the extraordinary archaeological sites of Epidaurus and Ancient Mycenae.

One week or more

Visit some of Athens' smaller, lesser-known museums, churches and galleries; take a day trip to the spectacular sanctuary at Delphi; catch a ferry from Piraeus and island-hop between Hydra, Spétses and other islands in the Saronic Gulf; hire a car and tour Marathon, Rámnous and other little-visited archaeological sites in Attica, or spend

Best One-day Excursions

- Cruise to the Saronic Gulf island of Aegina to visit the temple of Aphaia, one of the best-preserved Doric temples in Greece.
- Drive to Cape Soúnion to watch the sun set behind the Temple of Poseidon.
- Join a tour to Delphi, once regarded as the spiritual centre of the Greek world.
- Cruise to Hydra for a relaxing lunch on the picturesque waterfront.
- Drive to Corinth to see the ancient ruins and canal.

two or three days in the western Peloponnese exploring Ancient Olympia and the beautiful scenery of the Adriatic Coast.

Above: *Still commanding the city skyline, the Acropolis looms above Athens.*
Opposite: *The eastern façade of the Erechtheion, one of the magnificent temples on the Acropolis.*

The Acropolis

You have probably seen it a thousand times – even if you've never been to Athens. The Acropolis is a global icon of ancient culture, as instantly recognizable as Stonehenge or the Pyramids of Giza. And, yet, your first glimpse of the 'Sacred Rock', rising 90m (295ft) above the sprawling capital of Greece, will still send a prickle of anticipation down your spine. Simply translated, 'Acropolis' breaks down to *acro* (highest point) and *polis* (town) – but this says nothing of its towering achievements in architecture, nor its prime position as a place of worship and defence. To visit the ruins of the Acropolis is to wander through 5000 years of history and witness the very pinnacle of ancient Greek cultural and political supremacy.

Acropolis Checklist

Main entrance: off Dionysiou Areopagitou.
Nearest metro station: Akropoli.
Buses: 230, 231.
Opening hours May–Oct: 08:30–18:30 Mon–Fri, 08:30–15:00 Sat–Sun.
Opening hours Nov–Apr: 08:30–16:30 Mon–Fri, 08:30–15:00 Sat–Sun.
Full moon opening: once a year in Sep.
Closed: 1 Jan, 25 Mar, Easter Sunday, 1 May, 25–26 Dec.
Guided tours: available near main entrance.

History

The earliest evidence of human habitation on the Acropolis dates back to the Neolithic period around 3000BC. Some 1800 years later, there was a Mycenaean palace on the rock, fortified by Cyclopean walls. Then, in 510BC, the Delphic Oracle banned mere mortals, declaring the Acropolis a sacred place of the gods. Spiritual reverence, however, was in short supply 30 years later when the Persian forces of Xerxes razed every temple to the ground. Following the Greek victory over Persia, new defensive walls were constructed as the Acropolis entered its most spectacular building phase.

'We have forced every sea and land to be the highway of our daring, and everywhere… have left imperishable monuments behind us,' claimed Pericles, the mastermind behind the building boom of 447–432BC. Most of the monuments, including the Parthenon (dedicated to Athena, patron goddess of the city), date from this so-called Golden Age. Using Pentelic marble from a new quarry on Mount Pendéli, the work was carried out under the guidance of the great sculptor, Pheidias.

With Roman rule came new embellishments, such as the Theatre of Herodes Atticus, built on the southern slope of the Acropolis in the 2nd century AD. The decline of the Roman Empire exposed the Acropolis to attack, theft and vandalism. In AD267, the Gothic Heruli tribe wrought havoc. Then, under the Byzantine Empire, the Parthenon became a church with a bell tower. Following occupation by Ottoman Turks in the mid-15th century, it changed again – first to a mosque, complete with minaret, then to a gunpowder store. Rather inevitably, this latter reincarnation had explosive consequences. When the Venetians bombarded the Turks in 1687, a well-aimed cannon shot destroyed much of the building.

Following Greek Independence, modern Athenians began a zealous restoration project by removing any medieval and Ottoman structures that were still standing. An in-depth archaeological study of the ancient remains continues to the present day.

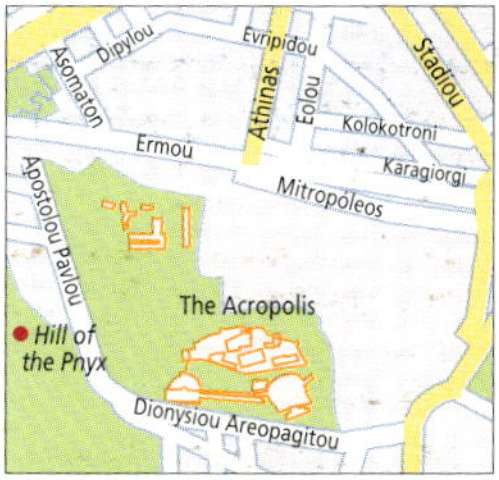

Acropolis Timeline

447–438BC Building of the Parthenon.
438–432BC Decoration of the Parthenon.
437–432BC Building of the Propylaia.
421–406BC Building of the Erechtheion.
420BC Building of the Temple of Athena Nike.
AD267 Parthenon interior destroyed by fire.
361–343 Parthenon repaired.
6th century Parthenon and Erechtheion converted to Christian churches.
12th century Propylaia used as a palace.
1456 Parthenon converted to a mosque.
1640 Explosion in the Propylaia.
1686 Temple of Athena Nike destroyed.
1687 Explosion in the Parthenon.
1801 Lord Elgin removes Parthenon friezes.
1835 First restoration of the Temple of Athena Nike.
1839–1863 First restorations of Erechtheion, Parthenon and Propylaia.
1975–ongoing Restoration under the supervision of the Committee for the Preservation of the Acropolis Monuments.

Losing Your Marbles

In 1801 Lord Elgin, the British Ambassador in Constantinople, acquired over 75m (246ft) of the Parthenon's friezes from the occupying Turks and sold them to the British Museum 15 years later for around £35,000. Much controversy has since surrounded the so-called Elgin Marbles, with famous names like Greek actress and politician, Melina Mercouri, campaigning vigorously for their return. With the construction of the new, purpose-built Acropolis Museum, the argument that these ancient treasures are more carefully preserved in London may no longer hold weight.

Exploring the Site

Before climbing the path to the Acropolis, pause for a moment's reflection. You are about to follow in the footsteps of the Panathenaic Procession when the residents of 5th century BC Athens marched through the city to the Acropolis. They bore a specially woven robe, or *peplos*, to drape over the shoulders of their patron goddess and would have walked through the grand temple gateway of the Propylaia. To their left towered a 9m (30ft) bronze statue of Athena Promachos, armed with shield and spear – so dazzling in the sunlight that she could be seen from ships sailing towards Athens. To the right of the Panathenaic Way, in the Sanctuary of Artemis Brauronia, stood a huge bronze depiction of the Trojan horse. But it was the Parthenon that drew the procession towards its climax. The great Doric temple was adorned with vividly coloured friezes, while inside stood a 12m (40ft) statue of Athena Parthenos, the Virgin, adorned with ivory and gold – one of the wonders of the ancient world.

Hold these images in your mind as you explore the Acropolis. The first entrance is the **Beulé Gate**, a Roman addition of the 3rd century AD. Walk along the southern edge of the **Propylaia** to view the **Temple of Athena Nike** before following the Panathenaic Way on to the Acropolis plateau. Measuring 4ha (10 acres), this area is dominated by the **Parthenon** and, to your left, the **Erechtheion**. Access to temple precincts is prohibited, but you can still admire these remarkable architectural monuments from the outside.

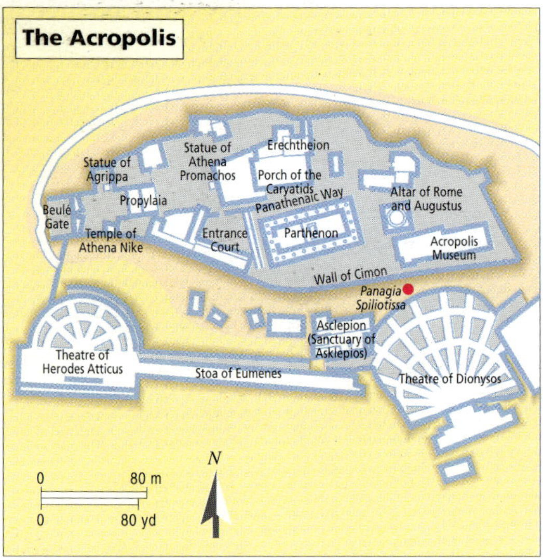

In the far southeast corner, you'll find the

Acropolis Museum which temporarily houses statues and friezes from the site. The **New Acropolis Museum** (*see* fact panel on page 34) will be located beneath the southern slope of the Acropolis and is due to be completed in time for the Athens 2004 Olympics.

Above: *The Propylaia forms a monumental gateway to the Acropolis.*

Before leaving through the Beulé Gate, spare a moment to admire the impressive city views from the Acropolis. To the north lie the districts of Pláka and Monastiráki; to the east is Kolonáki beneath the slopes of Lykavitós Hill; to the south is Philopáppou Hill (and distant views of the Saronic Gulf); to the west is the Hill of the Nymphs.

Beyond the Beulé Gate, head south of the rock by turning left out of the main entrance. After a short stroll you'll reach a viewpoint over the **Theatre of Herodes Atticus**.

The Propylaia ***

Built between 437 and 432BC, the Propylaia was designed by **Mnesikles** to form a monumental gateway to the Acropolis. The imposing temple-like structure was supported by rows of Ionic and Doric columns that channelled visitors through five doorways – the centremost of which led to the Panathenaic Way. To the left, a massive plinth, 8m (26ft) in height, once supported a statue of a charioteer. The north wing of the Propylaia housed an art gallery, the **Pinakothéke**, which also served as a chamber where VIPs could rest after the long climb. Greek travel writer, Pausanias, recorded seeing paintings here around AD150. Later, the Propylaia was used as an archbishop's residence, Frankish palace and Turkish fortress.

Acropolis Museum Star Exhibits

The Moschophoros (570BC): statue of a bearded man carrying a calf on his shoulders.
Rampin Rider (550BC): horseman statue used as a dedication to Athena.
The Peplos Kore (530BC): statue of a young woman (*kore*) wearing a peplos.
Mourning Athena (460BC): relief depiction of the goddess clad in a peplos.
Parthenon frieze (438–432BC): east section showing the gods Poseidon, Apollo, Artemis, Aphrodite and Eros.
The Caryatids (420BC): original statues of the women that supported the roof of the south porch of the Erechtheion.

Temple of Athena Nike ★★★

The history of this shrine to Athena Nike, the Warrior, is literally one of ups and downs. Built in 478BC from a design by **Kallikrates**, it was destroyed by Turks in 1687, reconstructed in 1835, dismantled and rebuilt in 1936, then taken down again in 2002. The latest restoration, using a titanium frame, should be complete by 2004. The temple stands on a 9.5m (31ft) bastion and has four Ionic columns of 4m (13ft) high. Fragments of a frieze (a replica) depicting the Battle of Plataiai (479BC) can still be seen, while the balustrade is adorned with a sculpture of Athena. According to legend, King Aegeus held vigil at the temple, waiting for his son, Theseus, to return from Crete. Theseus had set out to slay the Minotaur but, on his return to Athens, he forgot to signal his victory with a white sail. Devastated upon seeing a black one, King Aegeus threw himself off the precipice – immortalizing his name in the Aegean Sea.

NEW ACROPOLIS MUSEUM

Designed by **Bernard Tschumi**, a Swiss-born architect based in New York, the New Acropolis Museum will provide state-of-the-art displays of some of the world's most important antiquities. A glass gallery on top of the museum will showcase the **Parthenon Marbles** (including, it is hoped, the controversial sections that have been kept at the British Museum following Lord Elgin's 'acquisition' in 1801). The spectacular friezes will be reassembled using the same dimensions that they once occupied on the great temple itself. Located near the base of the south side of the Acropolis, the museum will also provide views of the Parthenon, as well as displays of early settlements that were excavated and sympathetically preserved during construction work.

The Parthenon ★★★

Without doubt one of the world's most famous ancient buildings, the Parthenon was designed by **Kallikrates** and **Iktinos**. Construction began in 447BC and finished in time for the Great Panathenaic Festival of 438BC (sculptural decoration was completed by 432BC). Dedicated to Athena Parthenos, the Virgin, it was built on the site of at least four earlier Parthenons.

As well as a shrine to Athena, the Parthenon served as a treasury for the Delian League (an alliance of some 200 Greek city-states formed in 478BC in fear of Persian attacks). Much of the temple, including the roof, the inner structure and 14 outer columns, was blown up during the Venetian siege of 1687 when the Turks were using the Parthenon as a powder magazine.

Apart from its wooden roof, the Parthenon was constructed entirely of Pentelic marble. Every aspect of its design, from the 46 ingeniously curved Doric columns to subtle bulges in the temple's base and steps, was intended to counteract the laws of perspective and create the illusion of perfect symmetry. Despite an estimated 13,400 blocks of marble, weighing up to 10 tons each, being used in its construction, the Parthenon has no straight lines.

A cult statue of Athena, clad with 44 talents of gold, stood in the east cella (or inner sanctum), while the exterior of the temple was lavishly decorated with colourful sculptures and friezes. The two pediments depicted the birth of Athena and the battle between the goddess and Poseidon (only fragments remain following a heavy-handed attempt by Morosini to take them to Venice). Sculptures on the entablature showed battles between the gods and giants on the east side, the Athenians and the Amazons on the west, the Lapiths and centaurs on the south and the Battle of Troy on the north.

Perhaps most famous of all, the Ionic frieze running 160m (524ft) along the exterior of all four walls of the cella portrayed the Panathenaic Procession – a remarkable scene of 400 humans and 200 animals designed in

Restoration of the Acropolis Monuments

Although excavation and restoration on the Acropolis has been ongoing since 1835, it was not until 1975 that major interventions were imposed to counter problems caused by centuries of damage from earthquakes, fires, bombardment, vandalism and, more recently, atmospheric pollution. Modern, highly technical approaches to restoration involve dismantling the restored or unstable parts of each monument, removing sculptures for safekeeping and replacing them with exact cast replicas, reassembling dismantled sections using authentic materials, and rectifying errors made in previous restorations.

Opposite: *Dating from the Archaic Period, the Moschophoros, or Calf-Bearer, is one of the many fine exhibits in the Acropolis Museum.*
Left: *View of the Parthenon, from the west.*

AREOPAGUS HILL

Well-worn (and slippery) marble steps lead to the top of Areopagus (Hill of Ares) from just below the Acropolis ticket office. In ancient times, the supreme court held trials here for murder, treason and corruption. It was also the site from where St Paul delivered his sermon in AD51 (the text is inscribed on a plaque near the steps). Nowadays, tourists climb to the top for stunning views across the Ancient Agora and the rooftops of Athens.

low relief by Pheidias. In 1816, Lord Elgin sold sections of these so-called Parthenon (or Elgin) Marbles to the British Museum (*see* fact panel on page 32). The New Acropolis Museum has been specifically designed to incorporate the missing pieces, adding to international pressure for their return to Athens.

The Erechtheion ***

Built between 421 and 406BC, the Erechtheion is located on the most sacred site of the Acropolis. It was here that Poseidon and Athena are said to have fought over who should become patron of the city. Poseidon struck the ground with his trident to create the salt spring Klepsydra, while Athena germinated the first olive tree and claimed victory (a small olive tree – though not the original – grows in the temple's western court). The main temple was dedicated to both Athena Polias and Erechtheus Poseidon – the two principal gods of Attica. It takes its name from Erechtheus, a mythical king of Athens who was part man, part snake. A relief frieze depicting the birth of Erechtheus once adorned the temple's exterior. His tomb, meanwhile, was located in the north porch – a particularly sacred spot fronted by six tall Ionic columns and a partly exposed roof and floor to reveal the marks left by Poseidon's trident.

Below: *Used in place of columns, these graceful caryatids support the south porch of the Erechtheion.*

This elegant building is famed for its caryatids (statues of women used as columns) that can be seen on the south porch – the so-called **Porch of the Caryatids**. In their pristine state, each one held a libation vessel – which suggests that they represented the priestesses, or *Arrephoroi*, who attended Athena. Four of the original caryatids are preserved in the Acropolis

Museum – the Erechtheion now has only replicas. Among the many roles the temple has played, perhaps the least auspicious was a Turkish harem and toilet in 1463. It was almost completely destroyed by cannon fire during the War of Independence in 1827.

Above: *Restored in 1955, the Theatre of Herodes Atticus is used today for outdoor concerts.*

The Theatres

Theatre of Herodes Atticus **

Built between AD161 and 174, and named after the Roman consul of the time, this small theatre (also called the Odeion of Herodes Atticus) was originally enclosed by a cedar roof that allowed for all-weather performances. Following restoration in the mid-1950s, it is now a magnificent venue for the summer **Festival of Athens** (*see* page 76) – an international extravaganza of concerts, theatre and ballet, with seating for around 5000. The theatre's impressive colonnade was once adorned with statues of the nine Muses. Along with many of Athens' monuments, it was badly damaged during the invasion of the Heruli in AD267.

Theatre of Dionysos **

Carved from the southeastern flank of the Acropolis around 330BC, the Theatre of Dionysos (open daily, 08:00–19:00 May–September, 08:00–17:00 October–April) was not only the first theatre built of stone, but it was also the birthplace of the Greek tragedy. Built on the site of an original 6th century BC wooden theatre, it was the venue of the famous Dionysia Festival, and great playwrights (including Aristophanes, Euripides and Sophocles) all had plays staged here. The Romans, who used the theatre as a gladiatorial arena, increased the seating capacity to 17,000 in 64 tiers. Only about 20 survive. The front rows of the auditorium were for VIPs only. One seat, reserved for the priest, Dionysos

Acropolis Study Centre

Located at 2–4 Makrygiánni, this research centre and storehouse for the Acropolis contains a scale model of the Parthenon and a plaster-cast replica of its frieze. It was closed for restoration following earthquake damage in 1999.

Eleutherios, still bears griffins and lion's paws. The theatre also boasts a fine stage front (Bema of Phaedros) depicting scenes from the life of Dionysos, the god of wine and merriment.

Above: *The Theatre of Dionysos was the birthplace of the Greek tragedy.*
Opposite: *Yuccas, euphorbias and other vegetation on Philopáppou Hill.*

Nearby are a number of sites worthy of perusal. **Panagía Spiliotissa**, a Byzantine chapel set into a cave above the theatre, was dedicated to the goddess Artemis and was where mothers brought their sick children. Below and a short distance to the west of the chapel, the **Sanctuary of Asklepios** (dedicated to the god of healing) was founded after 429BC when Athens was struck by plague. Donated by the wealthy benefactor, Eumenes II of Pergamon, the long colonnaded **Stoa of Eumenes** linked both theatres during Roman times and was a place where the audience could relax and drink between plays.

Hills to the West

Philopáppou Hill ★★

At 147m (482ft), Philopáppou Hill is the perfect vantage from which to admire the Acropolis – or gaze south towards Piraeus and the Saronic Gulf. The paved path, which leads to the summit, passes next to **Ágios Dimítrios Loumpardiáris**. This Byzantine church derives its name from an incident in 1656, when the congregation fell under the sights of a Turkish cannon stationed on the Acropolis. Before the weapon (known as Loumpárda) was fired, however, a heaven-sent bolt of lightning destroyed the weapon and killed the garrison commander.

Moonlight Opening

Key archaeological sites in Athens are opened to visitors during the full moon in September – a magical experience on a clear night. Moonlight concerts are also held in the Roman Agora. For more information check www.culture.gr

At the summit of Philopáppou Hill is the **Monument of Philopáppos**. Built in AD114–16, this marble tombstone is 12m (39ft) in height and decorated with a frieze showing Julius Antiochus Philopáppos arriving in Athens by chariot for his inauguration as Roman consul.

The **Dóra Strátou Theatre**, where folk-dance performances take place nightly in summer, is also located on the hill.

Hill of the Pnyx **

Smaller than Philopáppou and lying to the north, the Hill of the Pnyx was the meeting place of the *Ekklesia* (Democratic Assembly) in the 5th century BC. Among the great statesmen who addressed crowds of up to 18,000 from the *bema*, or speaker's platform, were Aristides, Demosthenes, Pericles and Themistocles. The assembly met up to 40 times a year and a minimum attendance of 5000 was required. Today, the hill is used for multilingual son et lumière shows.

Hill of the Nymphs *

North of the Pnyx lies another pine-clad hill reaching 103m (338ft) in height. The Hill of the Pnyx is the site of the **Asteroskopeíon** (Observatory) which was built in 1842 on the site of a sanctuary to nymphs.

PHOTOGRAPHY

The best light for photographing ancient sites and general city scenes is early morning or late afternoon when low-angle sunlight accentuates shadows and enriches colours and textures. Scenes can become quite 'flat' and washed-out under the harsh midday sun, although this may be the only time for taking shots in narrow streets which are otherwise in deep shadow. Remember always to ask permission when photographing local people (unless, of course, your subject matter is the evzone guards on parade outside the Parliament building). Taking pictures inside monasteries and many churches is forbidden and you will not be allowed to use a tripod or flash inside museums. Film is widely available in tourist shops across Athens.

ANCIENT AGORA

If the Acropolis was the sacred, lofty realm of the gods, then the Agora (entrance on Adrianoú, open daily, 08:00–19:00 May–September, 08:00–17:00 October–April) was where the nitty-gritty business of everyday mortal life was carried out in ancient Athens. Law courts, libraries, markets, a mint, a prison, schools, temples, theatres, and workshops crowded this hub of public life.

Themistocles (ca.528–462BC)

Background: Athenian statesman.
Achievements: developing Athens' navy and setting in place the Delian League.
Best known for: leading the Athenian fleet in the victory over the Persians at the Battle of Sálamis.

History

For some 850 years from 600BC, the Agora was the social, commercial, political and administrative heart of ancient Athens. It was here that Socrates expounded his theories on philosophy (before falling foul of the authorities who ordered his execution in 399BC). Barbarians ran riot following the fall of the Roman Empire and, centuries later, most traces of the Ancient Agora had been obscured by Byzantine buildings. In the 1930s the area was cleared when excavation by the American School of Classical Studies began.

Exploring the Site

From the main entrance, the **Altar of the Twelve Gods** is an appropriate place to begin your exploration. This small monument was where distances to all other points in the Greek world were measured. Follow the **Panathenaic Way** (that linked the Agora with the Acropolis) towards the central part of the Agora where you'll find the remains of the **Temple of Ares** and **Odeion of Agrippa** (an auditorium that could seat 1000 people). Bear right towards the site of the **Bouleuterion** (council chamber) and the **Metroön** (record office), beyond which lies Athens' best-preserved temple – the **Theseion** (or Temple of Hephaestus). Nearby are remnants of the **Tholos** (council headquarters) and the **Middle Stoa**. Another of the great colonnaded 'shopping arcades', the **Stoa of Attalos**, was recreated in the 1950s

and now houses the **Agora Museum**. If you're feeling slightly bewildered by this stage, get your bearings from the useful scale model inside. Finally, the southeast corner of the Agora is occupied by **Ágios Apóstoli**, an 11th-century church containing fine Byzantine frescoes.

Above: *Sculptures at the Agora Museum date from the 6th century* BC *to the 3rd century* AD.

Opposite: *In a corner of the Ancient Agora site is the fine Ágios Apóstoli.*

Stoa of Attalos ***

Recreated nearly 21 centuries after its first official opening in 138BC, this spectacular building faithfully replicates the long, shady porticoes and colonnaded, two-storey design of a typical arcade. Named after King Attalos of Pergamon, the original stoa would have housed 42 shops, as well as public latrines. The modern version contains the **Agora Museum** which displays artefacts from this complex site. Among the relics are some intriguing everyday objects, including a *klepsydra* (water clock) used for timing speeches and potsherds or *óstraka* used as voting tablets to ostracize any citizen who was regarded as a danger to the state. As long as 6000 people voted, then whoever got the most votes was exiled for 10 years. Also look out for the fragment of a rule book from one of Agora's libraries, some sandals and toys and a child's potty from the 4th century BC.

Temple of Hephaestus ***

Also known as the Theseion, this superbly preserved Doric temple was built in 449BC to honour the god of metalsmiths. Boasting 34 columns, it uses similar design trickery to create the illusion of perfection that was employed in the Parthenon. A frieze on the entablature depicts the *Twelve Labours of Heracles* (*see* fact panel on page 12). Surrounding the temple is a garden with the kind of medicinal and herbal plants that ancient Greeks may have grown. Converted into a church in AD1300, the temple persisted through turbulent Ottoman times, performing its last service in 1834. It was then used as Greece's first archaeological museum.

ATHENIAN PHILOSOPHERS

Aristotle (384–322BC) Scientific genius.
Diogenes (c400–325BC) Founder of the Cynics.
Epicurus (341–270BC) Developed the theory of a materialist universe.
Euclid (ca.300BC) Mathematician famed for his textbook, *Elements*, on geometry.
Plato (429–347BC) Most renowned for his work, *The Republic*, a long enquiry into the best form of life for people and states.
Socrates (469–399BC) Exploring the question of how men should conduct their lives, Socrates was hugely influential – particularly on Plato.

Pláka and Monastiráki

You could easily spend several days delving into these historic districts lying to the north of the Acropolis. Between them, they have a liberal scattering of museums and churches, plenty of shopping opportunities (such as the famous flea market), plus several historic monuments (including the remains of the largest temple ever built in Greece). If, however, you are feeling somewhat jaded after taking in the archaeological sites of the Acropolis and the Ancient Agora, then you'll find abundant cafés, bars and tavernas in which to recharge your batteries and plan your next round of sightseeing.

Great Dionysia

An annual five-day theatrical contest, Great Dionysia was a highlight in the social calendar of ancient Athens. On day one, participants paraded hundreds of cows and bulls destined to be sacrificed to the god, Dionysos. His cult statue was brought from Eleutherai to watch the proceedings. On the second day, Athens' allies made tributes of silver, treaties were announced and special honours accorded before the theatrical plays began. These consisted of tragedies and satires until the final day when comedies were performed. Well over a thousand men and boys took part in the plays each year.

Exploring the Area

About 1km (0.6 mile) west of Plateía Monastiráki (but close to Thissio metro station) is the ancient cemetery of **Kerameikós**. A burial ground may not immediately strike you as a 'must-see', but this is, nevertheless, a fascinating, green and peaceful corner of Athens. Eastwards is the **flea market** (centred on Plateía Avissynías), **Hadrian's Library**, the **Roman Agora** and **Anafiótika** – a maze of old houses tucked up against the Acropolis. Nearby is **Plateía Lysikrátous** with its intriguing monument. The triumphal **Hadrian's Arch** is just a short distance to the southeast and leads to the mighty **Temple of Olympian Zeus**. Strolling between these landmarks, you will encounter several **churches** and **museums** – all worth a visit if you have the time!

Kerameikós **

Named after the potters (*kerameis*) who once worked on the local clay deposits along the banks of the River Eridanos, Kerameikós (148 Ermoú, open daily, 08:00–19:00 May–September, 08:00–17:00 October–April) contains the remains of two ceremonial entranceways. The most important was the **Dípylon Gate**, constructed in 478BC. Guarded by two towers and boasting a large courtyard, this was literally the front door of ancient Athens and marked the starting point of the Panathenaic Way to the Ancient Agora and Acropolis. Built around the same time, the **Sacred Gate** led west to Eleusis along the pilgrimage route of the Sacred Way (*see* page 96).

Kerameikós is best known, however, as the site of an ancient cemetery with burials dating from the 12th century BC. Many of Athens' elite and wealthy were buried along **The Street of the Tombs** where most of the remaining graves and monuments are found. These include some beautifully ornate stelae (relief sculptures) – the Stele of Demetria and Pamphile is particularly striking – as well as an imposing marble bull on the tomb of Dionysos of Kollytos, a rich Athenian treasurer. The original is in the **Oberländer Museum** near the site entrance – along with a collection of artefacts ranging from black-figure funerary vases to small terracotta toys from children's graves.

Opposite: *Aeropagus Hill provides a spectacular vantage from which to admire the Temple of Hephaestus in the Ancient Agora.*
Below: *The Stele of Dexileos commemorates a young man killed in 394BC during the Corinthian War.*

Hadrian's Library *

In its heyday around the 2nd century AD, Hadrian's Library would have been a grand affair measuring 120m (394ft) by 80m (262ft) and graced with 100 columns and a pool. Although the ruins are not open to the public, you can still view part of the west wall from Areos Street.

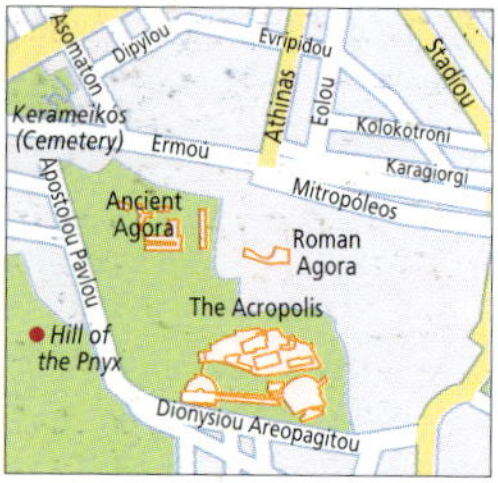

The Museum of Traditional Greek Ceramics, also known as Kyriazópoulos Folk Ceramic Museum (*see* page 52), is located in the adjacent Tsistaráki Mosque, while **Pantánassa church**, the 'little monastery' (*see* page 49) is across the square.

Roman Agora **

Although much of this Agora (open daily, 08:30–19:00 May–September, 08:00–17:00 October–April) lies hidden beneath Pláka, the remains of Athens' Roman civic centre are still worth a visit. Excavations have revealed a large building measuring 111m (364ft) by 98m (322ft). It consisted of a central courtyard surrounded by stoas containing shops and storerooms. One of the most visible remains is a monumental entranceway, the **Gate of Athena Archegetis**, built between 19 and 11BC with a donation from Julius Caesar. Other nearby buildings included the Agoranomion (dedicated to Emperor Augustus) and the Vespasianae – a 68-seat public latrine from the 1st century AD which comprised a square hall with benches bearing holes.

Below: *This impressive wall, built around AD132, is the most visible remains of Hadrian's Library.*

The most interesting monument on the site, however, is the octagonal **Tower of the Winds**, a multipurpose sundial, water clock, weather vane and compass designed by the astronomer, Andronikos, around 150–125BC. Its name comes from the eight winds, personified in friezes, on each compass-orientated side of the tower. Blowing from the north is icy Boreas; easterly Apeliotes bears fruit and corn; southerly Notos carries a pitcher of water, while the gentle westerly wind of Zephyros scatters flowers.

Standing over 12m (39ft) in height with a diameter of 8m (26ft), the tower once held a bronze triton weather vane. Beneath the friezes are metal rods which cast shadows across etched sundial lines. Scant traces of the water clock, in the form of a circular channel, can be seen inside the tower which, during the mid-18th century, was used as a retreat for Muslim dervishes.

Above: *The extraordinary Tower of the Winds dominates a corner of the Roman Agora site. Each of its eight sides depicts a different wind.*

Surrounded by orange trees in another corner of the Roman Agora site, **Fethiye Djami Mosque** was constructed in 1456 on the ruins of an early Christian church and is one of the few remaining buildings in Athens from the Ottoman occupation.

From the Roman Agora, head towards the Acropolis for **Anafiótika** (*see* page 46), **Kanellópoulos Museum** (*see* page 50) and the **University of Athens Museum** (*see* page 52), or bear north and east to find the **Museum of Greek Popular Musical Instruments** (*see* page 51), the **Mitrópoli** and the church of **Panagía Gorgoepíkoös** (*see* page 48–49).

What Wind Where?

Although weathered by time and the elements, the frieze on the Roman Agora's **Tower of the Winds** still clearly depicts the following eight winds: **Boreas** (north), **Kaikias** (northeast), **Apeliotes** (east), **Euros** (southeast), **Notos** (south), **Lips** (southwest), **Zephyros** (west) and **Skiron** (northwest).

Anafiótika **

Snug against the Acropolis, Anafiótika is a tangle of narrow, largely car-free, streets hemmed in by whitewashed houses with balconies decorated with bougainvillea and bright pots of geraniums. It is a scene more reminiscent of a typical Cycladic village than a city centre.

Anafiótika is bounded by two 17th-century churches – **Ágios Geórgios** to the south and **Ágios Simeón** to the north – as well as the charming Byzantine chapel of **Ágios Nikólaos Ragavás** (*see* page 48).

Plateía Lysikrátous **

Erected around 335BC, the **Monument of Lysikrátous**, which dominates this square, is a fine and rare example of a choragic monument. These were built to honour winners of the annual choral festival held at the Theatre of Dionysos (*see* page 37). Named after its wealthy sponsor, this elaborate domed structure, comprising six Corinthian columns and a finial of acanthus leaves, would originally have supported a bronze tripod. A frieze above the columns depicted Dionysos and the Tyrrhenian pirates. Many centuries later, the monument served as the library for a Capuchin friary in which Byron reputedly wrote part of his epic poem, *Childe Harold*, in 1810.

Hadrian's Arch *

This triumphal arch was built in AD131 to mark the boundary between what Emperor Hadrian saw as 'old'

HADRIAN (AD76–138)

Background: Roman emperor 117–38.
Achievements: Promoting good government and securing the frontiers of the Roman Empire.
Best known for: instigating many fine building programmes, including several monuments in Athens.

and 'new'. An inscription on the Acropolis side reads, 'This is Athens, the ancient city of Theseus', while on the other side it states, 'This is the city of Hadrian, and not of Theseus.'

Temple of Olympian Zeus ***

Measuring over 96m (315ft) long and 40m (131ft) wide, this was the largest temple ever built in Greece – dwarfing even the Parthenon. Dedicated to Zeus Olympios, it took several attempts, spanning some 700 years, to complete. Peisistratos the Younger began the process around 515BC, with Antiochus IV Epiphanes, King of Syria, making another attempt in 174BC. But it was not until the reign of Emperor Hadrian that the temple was finally finished in time for the Panhellenic Festival of AD132. It must have been a magnificent sight – 104 columns each measuring 17m (56ft) in height surrounding an inner sanctum in which stood a gold and ivory statue of Zeus.

Only 15 columns remain today, each one characterized by an elegant Corinthian capital that replaced simple Doric ones in 174BC in the course of the temple's protracted creation. One tumbled during a gale in 1852 and has been left where it fell.

Other excavations at the site have revealed the remains of the **Temple of Apollo Delphinios** (500BC), parts of the **old city walls** (479BC) and **Roman baths** (AD131–132).

LYSIKRÁTOUS MONUMENT

Despite Lord Elgin's attempts to remove it, this 4th century BC structure is the city's only intact choragic monument. A frieze near the top depicts a battle between the theatrical god, Dionysos, and Tyrrhenian pirates. Below is an inscription which reads, 'Lysikrátous of Kikynna, son of Lysitheides, was choragus; the tribe of Akamantis won the victory with a chorus of boys; Theon played the flute; Lysiades, an Athenian, trained the chorus; Evainetos was archon'.

Opposite: *One of the many churches in Anafiótika.*
Left: *The Monument of Lysikrátous with the Acropolis looming behind.*

Technopolis

Located near Kerameikós at 100 Pireos, Technopolis (open 09:00–21:00 Mon–Fri) occupies a redeveloped 1862 gas factory and contains exhibitions on culture, industry and technology.

Churches

Ágios Nikólaos Ragavás **

A popular wedding venue, this 11th-century Byzantine chapel was built using marble columns and other remains of ancient buildings. Its bell was the first to ring out after liberation from the Turks in 1833 and the Germans in 1944. Corner of Prytaneíou and Epichármou, open 08:00–12:00, 17:00–20:00 daily.

Kapnikaréa *

Rising from a square in the middle of a busy shopping street, 11th-century Kapnikaréa was rescued from demolition in 1834 through intervention by King Ludwig of Bavaria. It was restored in the 1950s by the University of Athens and contains modern frescoes by Fótis Kóntoglou. Corner of Kapnikaréa and Ermoú, open 08:00–14:00 Monday, Wednesday, Saturday; 08:00–12:30, 17:00–19:30 Tuesday, Thursday, Friday; 08:00–11:30 Sunday.

Opposite: *Modern mosaics adorn the entrance to the Mitrópoli.*
Below: *The Temple of Olympian Zeus once boasted 104 columns.*

Mitrópoli **

Dedicated to Evangelismós Theotókou (the Annunciation of the Virgin), Athens Cathedral consumed

marble from over 70 demolished churches during its construction from 1840–60. Adorned with a fine mosaic of the Annunciation above its entrance, the Mitrópoli covers an area of 40m (131ft) by 20m (66ft) and reaches a height of 24m (79ft). Inside are the tombs of two saints, Ágia Filothéi and Gregory V – both murdered by Ottoman Turks. Plateía Mitropóleos, open 06:30–19:00 daily.

Panagía Gorgoepíkoös ***

In contrast to its giant neighbour, Panagía Gorgoepíkoös or 'Little Cathedral' is just 7.5m (25ft) long by 12m (40ft) wide. What it lacks in scale, however, it more than compensates for with historical and architectural significance. Dating from the 12th century, this domed church (dedicated to the Madonna who Swiftly Hears) incorporates relief sculptures and other fragments of ancient and early Christian monuments. The frieze on the lintel above the main entrance dates from the 4th century BC. Plateía Mitropóleos, open 07:00–19:00 daily.

Pantánassa *

Believed to have been built in the 10th century, this is the 'little monastery', or *monastiráki*, which gave the area its name. East side of Plateía Monastiráki.

Russian Church of the Holy Trinity *

Also known as Ágios Nikodímos, this 11th-century church was restored by Tsar Alexander II during the 1850s. Located at 21 Filellínon, open 07:30–10:00 Monday–Friday; 07:00–11:00 Saturday and Sunday.

Athens for Children

The **Hellenic Children's Museum**, 14 Kydathinaíon, open 09:30–13:30 Mon–Wed, 09:30–13:30 and 17:00–20:00 Fri, has plenty of interactive displays and activities to keep children entertained for hours.
The **Museum of Greek Children's Art**, 9 Kodrou, open 10:00–14:00 Tue–Sat, 11:00–14:00 Sun, exhibits paintings inspired by an annual children's competition and hosts regular art workshops for youngsters.

Above: *Built entirely of Pentelic marble, Panagía Gorgoepíkoös is known locally as Mikrí Mitrópoli, or 'Little Cathedral'.*

Museums

Centre of Folk Art & Tradition *

Located at the home of folklorist Angelikis Hatzimichalis, this interesting centre conjures up images of the past through recreations of traditional Greek lifestyles. Located at 6 Angelikis Hatzimichalis, open 09:00–13:00, 17:00–21:00; 09:00–13:00 Saturday and Sunday.

Frissíras Museum *

With a mixture of permanent and temporary exhibitions, this museum houses a collection of 20th-century art by Greek and foreign artists. Located at 3–7 Monís Asteríou, open 11:00–19:00 Wednesday–Friday, 10:00–15:00 Saturday and Sunday.

Greek Folk Art Museum **

Showcasing everything from shadow puppets and festival masks to needlework and carving, the Greek Folk Art Museum also has some splendid masquerade costumes, including the famous masked goat dancer of Skyros (17 Kydathineon, open 10:00–14:00 Tuesday–Sunday).

Jewish Museum of Greece *

Tracing the history of the nation's Jewish community from the 3rd century BC, this museum includes shocking and moving insights into the Holocaust when nearly 90% of Greece's Jewish population was exterminated. Located at 39 Níkis, open 09:00–14:30 Monday–Friday, 10:00–14:00 Sunday, closed Saturday.

Kanellópoulos Museum **

Occupying a beautifully restored 1884 mansion, this museum houses the extensive private collection of the Kanellópoulos family. It includes such treasures as Mycenaean figurines, Persian jewellery from the 5th

Byzantine Icons

Icon painters are concentrated in the Pláka area of Athens – especially in the streets just south of Plateía Mitropóleos. Some artists still use traditional materials (egg-based tempera on wood). Saints can be painted to order – you just need to supply a photograph for the artist to work from.

century BC, Attic vases and Byzantine icons, as well as weapons, coins and portraits from throughout the Hellenistic world. Corner of Theorías and Pános, open 08:30–15:00 Tuesday–Sunday.

Museum of Greek Popular Musical Instruments **

Displays of numerous instruments dating from the 18th century feature here, including a collection of over 1200 from Cretan musicologist Phoebus Anogianákis. Headphones let you sample music from instruments as diverse as Greek goatskin bagpipes, a bouzouki and a lute. There is also a collection of church bells in the basement, while music recitals are sometimes held in the gardens. Located at 1–3 Diogenous, open 10:00–14:00 Tuesday, Thursday–Sunday, 12:00–18:00 Wednesday, closed Monday.

Five Great Byzantine Churches

1. Dáfní Monastery, west of Athens
2. Kaisarianí Monastery, Mount Ymittós
3. Kapnikaréa, Ermoú Street, Athens
4. Ágios Dimitrios Loumpardiáris, Philopáppou Hill
5. Ágios Apóstoli, Ancient Agora

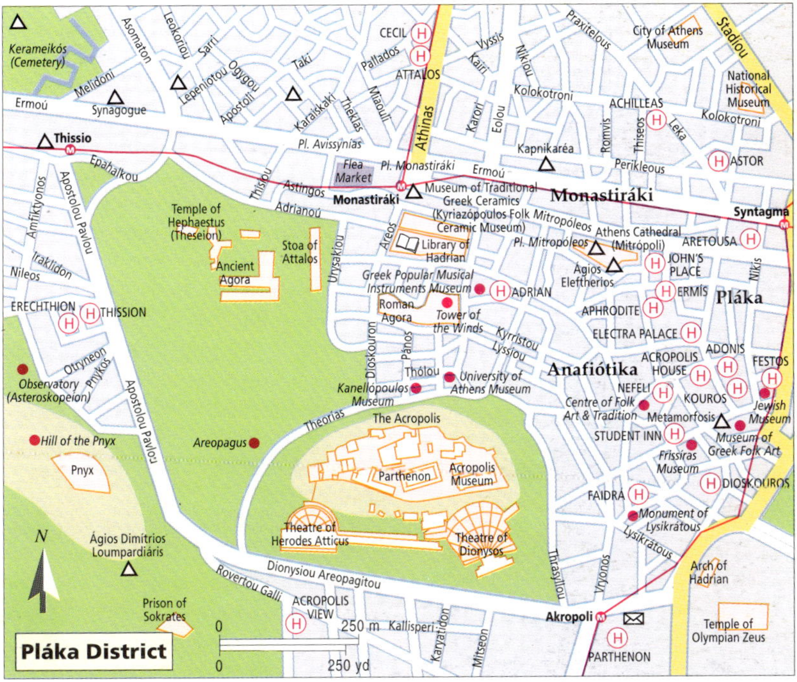

Bouzouki

One of the most popular of Greek traditional instruments, the bouzouki belongs to the lute family. It is plucked with a plectrum and is often used to play traditional Rembetika music.

Museum of Traditional Greek Ceramics ★★

Also known as Kyriazópoulos Folk Ceramic Museum (after the professor who donated many of the 20th-century jugs, jars and earthenware on display), this museum is located in an equally fascinating restored mosque. During its construction in 1759, the Turkish governor, Tsistarákis, needed lime for the mosque's stucco work, so he ordered one of the columns of the Temple of Olympian Zeus to be dynamited. He was exiled the same year. Located at 1 Areos, open 09:00–14:30 Monday and Wednesday–Sunday.

University of Athens Museum ★

The original home of the city's university during the 1830s, this museum contains academic memorabilia, such as technical instruments, maps and portraits of old professors. Located at 5 Thólou, open 14:30–19:00 Monday and Wednesday; 09:30–14:30 Tuesday, Thursday and Friday.

Below: *The ornate neo-classical entrance to the Kanellópoulos Museum.*

Eating Out and Shopping

Pláka and Monastiráki are a magnet for locals and visitors in search of food, drink, nightlife and shopping. The most famous shopping venue is the **flea market** (open daily, but busiest from 07:00–15:00 on Sunday) which is centred on Plateía Avissynías. Here, you will find dozens of stalls selling everything from glassware, furniture and copper pots to oddities like an antiquated diving helmet or gramophone. Old men arrive, pushing carts laden with coins, books and stamps, while on the nearby streets of **Adrianoú** and **Pandrósou** there are shops crammed with imitation black-

figure vases, t-shirts, postcards and other curios.

One of the best all-round shopping streets is **Ermoú** (named after Hermes, the patron of commerce) which runs from Monastiráki towards Syntagma Square. Partly pedestrianized, its shops offer complete retail therapy – from shoes and leather goods to clothes and jewellery.

You will never go hungry in Pláka and Monastiráki – both districts are riddled with tavernas and bars. Some of the most atmospheric places to eat are along **Adrianoú** (opposite the Ancient Agora), **Plateía Lysikrátous** (overlooking the choragic monument), **Plateía Mitropóleos** (beneath the cathedral), **Anafiótika** (with views across the Ancient Agora) and the streets surrounding the **Roman Agora**.

Above: *Looking for bargains at the flea market in Monastiráki.*

Syntagma

Lying at the hub of this city-centre district to the north-east of Pláka is Plateía Syntágmatos (Syntagma or Constitution Square). With its modern metro station, fountains and seats, the square is a popular meeting place for locals and tourists alike. The busy Amalías Avenue running along its eastern edge is the final stop for the E95 airport bus. Most new arrivals, however, barely give Syntagma a second glance before hurrying off towards the Acropolis and Agora. But when 'ancient monument fever' subsides, Syntagma is well worth a more detailed perusal.

Exploring the Area

For people-watching, you can't beat **Syntagma Square**. In the square itself, you'll see lottery-ticket vendors and bread-ring sellers, while on the courtyard in front of the

Alexander the Great (356–323BC)

Background: King of Macedon (363–323BC).
Achievements: building a mighty empire across Europe, Asia Minor and beyond.
Best known for: being the greatest general and imperialist conqueror of antiquity.

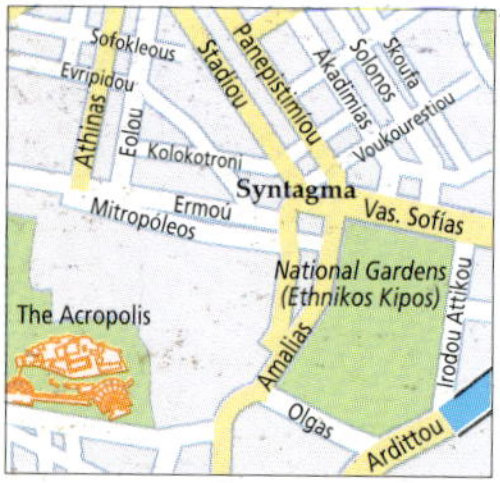

Parliament (Voulí), there is always a pair of evzone National Guards patrolling in front of the **Monument to the Unknown Soldier**. Even if you don't intend using the metro, **Syntagma Metro Station** is a quirky 'must-see' with its fascinating display of archaeological finds uncovered during the station's excavation. Venturing from the square, you can delve into the maze of paths that thread through the tranquil **National Gardens** or take in some of Athens' architectural gems – the **Academy**, **University** and **National Library** to the north, and the **Záppeion** exhibition hall and **Kallimármaro Stadium** to the south. And, of course, you are never far away from a museum.

The Parliament **

Dominating Syntagma Square, the neoclassical Parliament building was built from 1836–1840 and originally served as a palace for King Otto. It became the seat of the Greek parliament in 1935 and also houses the **Monument to the Unknown Soldier**. Etched with a relief of a fallen Greek warrior, the tomb is guarded round the clock by a pair of evzones. Dressed in the traditional uniform of the klephts (mountain fighters during the War of Independence), the evzones' exaggerated marching manoeuvres are as elaborate as their costumes of short kilts and pom-pom shoes. Every hour, on the hour, the guard is changed, while at 11:00 on Sundays a full ceremony unfolds in front of the tomb.

Opposite: *Exotic palms at the National Gardens.*
Below: *High-stepping evzones continuously parade in front of the Monument to the Unknown Soldier.*

National Gardens *

When the traffic gets too much or you simply want

to find a shady bench on which to relax, the main entrances to the National Gardens are just a short stroll from the Parliament. Formerly known as the Royal Gardens, this 16ha (40-acre) park was ordered by Queen Amalía in the 1840s. Paths lead to ornamental ponds and quiet clearings adorned with modern statues. There are also children's play areas and a small **Botanical Museum**, while a café can be found off Irodou Attikou. Standing in adjacent formal gardens to the south is the **Záppeion** conference centre – an impressive late 19th-century building that was used as the headquarters of the 1896 Olympic Committee. Also nearby is the **Presidential Palace** which was home to the Royal Family from 1890–1967 before becoming the official residence of the President.

Kallimármaro (Old Olympic) Stadium **

Although not strictly in the district of Syntagma, this magnificent marble stadium is just across Leoforos Konstantinou Road which skirts the southeast corner of the National Gardens. Measuring 204m (669ft) in length and 83m (272ft) in width, Kallimármaro Stadium (also known simply as Stádio) can hold up to 60,000 spectators

Stamp Collectors

Located near Kallimármaro Stadium, the **Philatelic Museum** is open 08:00–20:00 Mon and Wed, 08:00–14:00 Tue, Thu and Fri.

Above: *The huge marble Kallimármaro Stadium was the venue for the first modern Olympics in 1896.*

in 47 rows of seats. It was the venue of the first modern Olympic Games on 5 April 1896 – but the athletic history of this site dates back much further.

The original Panathenaic Stadium was built here by Lykourgos around 330BC. Hadrian oversaw its first renovation in the 1st century AD when it was used for gladiatorial contests. However, it was the wealthy Roman benefactor Herodes Atticus who foot the bill for its later reconstruction (using Pentelic marble) in time for the Panathenaic games of AD144. Over the centuries that followed, the stadium gradually fell into disrepair. Its graceful, curved tiers of marble seats were chiselled away for use in other buildings or to make lime. Fortunately, the 2nd-century geographer Pausanias described the stadium in his *Guide to Greece*, and it was this text that helped inspire the design of today's replica.

First Cemetery of Athens

Located near Kallimármaro Stadium and open 07:30–18:00 daily, the First Cemetery of Athens (not to be confused with the much older Kerameikós) is the final resting place for many famous names in recent Greek history. Tombs include those of German archaeologist, Heinrich Schliemann, Nobel prize-winning poet, Giórgos Seféris, benefactor, Antónis Benákis, and actress and politician Melina Mercouri. Near the entrance there is a bronze memorial (*The Mother of the Occupation*) to the 40,000 Athenians who perished through starvation during World War II.

The Neoclassical Trilogy **

Head north from Syntagma Square along Panepistimíou Street and you'll soon encounter a remarkable architectural trio on your right. The first of these 19th-century neoclassical landmarks is the **Athens Academy**. Athena and Apollo stand atop Ionic columns, while statues of Socrates and Plato sit on either side of the steps leading to this exquisite building with its pediments crammed with yet more sculptures. Next door is the **University of Athens**, another masterpiece of Pentelic marble, while the **National Library**, designed like a Doric temple, completes the trilogy.

Behind the trilogy, at 50 Akadimías, is the **City of Athens Cultural Centre**, a useful source of information on events and exhibitions.

Museums

City of Athens Museum ★

Displaying royal memorabilia, including furniture and paintings, this former palace was the home of King Otto and Queen Amalía during the 1830s. There is also an interesting scale model of 19th-century Athens and the manuscript of the 1843 Constitution (7 Paparigópoulou, open 09:00–13:30 Monday, Wednesday, Friday–Sunday).

National Historical Museum ★

Prior to being opened as a museum in 1961, this neoclassical building was the site of the first Greek parliament. It now contains chronological exhibits tracing Greek history from Byzantine times to the 20th century. The War of Independence features prominently with displays of Byron's helmet and sword, as well as other weapons and costumes. Outside the museum is a statue of General Theódoros Kolokotrónis on horseback. Located at 13 Stadíou, open 09:00–14:00 Tuesday–Sunday.

Numismatic Museum ★

This fine neoclassical mansion (designed by Ernst Ziller) was the former home of Heinrich Schliemann, the renowned archaeologist who excavated Troy and Mycenae. Today it houses a collection of 600,000 coins and traces the history of money. Located at 12 Panepistimíou, open 08:30–14:30 Tuesday–Sunday.

Theatre Museum ★

Celebrating Greek theatrical history from classical dramas to present day, this small museum contains costumes, posters, props, a puppet theatre and displays on famous names, such as actress Melina Mercouri. Located at 50 Akadimías, open 09:00–15:00 Monday–Friday.

Syntagma Metro

Well worth a visit even if you are not planning to take a train, Syntagma Metro is a veritable museum of Athenian history. Excavation of the underground station in the early 1990s turned into the country's biggest ever archaeological dig. Artefacts and ruins dating from the classical period to the 19th century were uncovered. They included an aqueduct, bronze foundries, a late Roman bath complex, early Christian and Byzantine churches and a section of Amalias Street from the reign of King Otto. Although many of the finds are held at the university, the metro station contains a well-presented and informative display.

Below: *Athena, Socrates and Plato are just a few of the statues adorning the imposing neoclassical Athens Academy.*

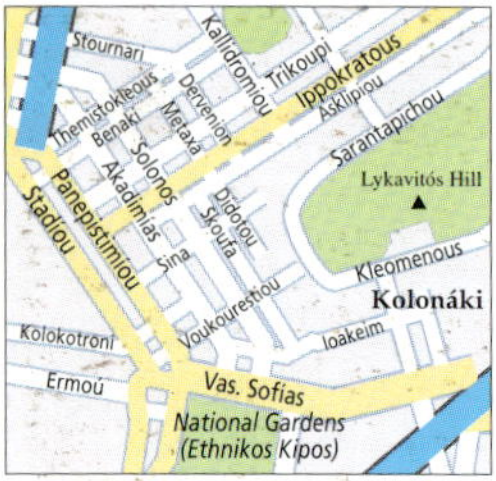

Kolonáki and Lykavitós

Nestled beneath the southern slopes of Lykavitós Hill, the district of Kolonáki oozes style. Its streets are lined with chic designer boutiques, pavement cafés and trendy bars. This is the place to go window-shopping or to sip *frappé* (iced coffee) alongside affluent Athenians. That's not to say, however, that Kolonáki lacks any cultural interest. Far from it. The museums in this area include some of the city's finest, while the views from Lykavitós Hill are unrivalled.

Exploring the Area

Plateía Kolonakíou lies at the heart of this fashionable quarter. Named after the ancient column (*kolonáki*) that was found here, the square is tucked away down a side street leading off Vassilísis Sofías. This wide avenue has the so-called 'museum mile', beginning with the **Benáki Museum** and continuing east with the **Goulandrís Museum of Cycladic and Ancient Greek Art**, the **Byzantine and Christian Museum**, the **War Museum** and, finally, the **National Gallery of Art**. Don't expect to notch up the entire mile in one session. The first two museums are particularly outstanding and easily warrant a day between them.

Below: *A floodlit bell tower at the top of Lykavitós Hill.*

Lykavitós Hill ★★

Towering behind Kolonáki, this 277m (909ft) hill provides spectacular panoramic views over greater Athens. Those with the energy can walk to the top (a path climbs through cypress and pine trees and the trek should take about one hour). Alternatively, a much quicker funicular railway operates daily from Ploutárchou Street and departs every 10 minutes (less often during winter), 08:00–23:45.

The whitewashed 19th-century chapel of **Ágios Geórgios** dominates the summit of Lykavitós and looks especially

Above: *Night-time view towards the Acropolis from Lykavitós Hill.*

dramatic when floodlit at night. Every Easter, it is the starting point for a candlelit procession that winds down the wooded slopes to the city below.

Surrounding the chapel are observation decks with mounted telescopes enabling you to zoom in on the Acropolis, the Temple of Olympian Zeus and other city landmarks visible from the hill. On a clear day (if the pollution and haze allow) you should be able to see as far as the Saronic Gulf and even the island of Aegina.

Lykavitós Hill has a restaurant and a couple of cafés, as well as the open-air **Lykavitós Theatre** where classical, jazz and rock concerts are held during summer.

Museums

Benáki Museum ***

The former home of the Benákis family, this superb museum was founded in 1930 by Antónis Benákis, the son of a wealthy Greek merchant who made his fortune in Alexandria. It contains a significant and diverse collection based on Benákis' personal acquisitions in Eurasia, as well as several major donations. Over 20,000 items, ranging from sculptures and paintings to jewellery and costumes, are arranged chronologically over four floors.

The ground floor covers prehistory to the late Roman Period, the Byzantine Empire and post-Byzantine

Archimedes (ca.287–212BC)

Background: Greek mathematician and inventor.
Achievements: discovering, among other things, the law of hydrostatics (*Archimedes' principle*).
Best known for: allegedly running through the streets shouting 'Eureka!' when he made this discovery.

Above: *The Benáki Museum houses a diverse collection of Greek arts and crafts.*

centuries. As you peruse the well-presented display cabinets, look out for **Cycladic figurines** (2600–2500BC), **Mycenaean jewellery** from Thebes, large **Attic amphorae** from the Geometric Period (around 700–750BC), **Corinthian vases** (7th–6th century BC) mass-produced as perfume vials, and gold jewels from the Hellenistic **Treasure of Thessaly**. Some of the most important legacies of ancient painting – the **El Fayum portraits** – are next. Named after the Egyptian oasis where they were discovered, these strangely hypnotic artworks date from the 3rd century AD.

Intricate mosaics and illuminated manuscripts are displayed nearby, but you will no doubt be drawn on towards the stunning collection of **Byzantine icons**. One of the most arresting of these brilliantly coloured paintings is a 15th-century depiction of St Ann and the Virgin.

The first floor focuses on the development of Hellenism during the period of Ottoman rule and also contains galleries depicting ecclesiastical art from the post-Byzantine period. The entrance to the gallery is dominated by a late **17th-century map** of Greece (executed in egg tempera on wood) showing Venice's efforts to repossess territory annexed by the Ottoman Turks. There are also two lavishly **wood-panelled rooms** from an 18th-century mansion in Kozáni.

The second floor portrays culture, economy and society on the eve of the War of Independence. This is also where you will find any special temporary exhibitions, as well as a popular café overlooking the National Gardens.

The third floor covers Independence and the formation of the modern Greek State and includes portraits of Greek heroes and some interesting memorabilia such as Byron's portable desk and the original score of the Greek national anthem.

Greek Vases

From ca.1100BC to Hellenistic times, Athens was a major pottery centre. During this period, three distinctive styles emerged. **Geometric** vases, with abstract patterns and regimented human figures, predominated between 1000 and 770BC; The **black-figure** style, where more graceful figures were painted using black liquid clay on iron-rich red clay vases, was first used ca.700BC. **Red-figure** vases began to appear ca.530BC. These often depicted mythological scenes with figures outlined with black glaze.

Located at 1 Koumbari, open 09:00–17:00 Monday, Wednesday, Friday–Saturday; 09:00–24:00 Thursday; 09:00–15:00 Sunday.

Goulandrís Museum of Cycladic and Ancient Greek Art ***

The simplistic, yet mesmerizing, marble figurines in this remarkable museum provide striking evidence of a culture that flourished in the Cyclades islands from 3200–2000BC. Opened in 1986 with an initial collection from the Goulandrí shipping family, the Museum of Cycladic Art contains over 300 objects from this little-known civilization. The most enigmatic of the exhibits in the first floor **Cycladic Art Collection** are the **female figurines** (nude with arms folded over the belly) and the rarer **male figurines**. The latter are often shown performing a specific activity – the **Toastmaster** (ca.2800–2300BC) depicts a seated man raising a cup as if proposing a toast. **Cycladic pots**, including the mysterious 'frying pans', are also on display. Whether these curious artefacts were used as drums, with skins stretched over them, or receptacles for offerings to the dead, is still being debated.

The second floor of the museum houses the **Ancient Greek Art Collection** with displays of pottery, terracotta figurines, sculpture, coins and jewellery. Tucked away in a corner is a delightful amphora still covered in worm casts and oyster shells from a time when it lay, undiscovered, on the sea bed.

The third floor has temporary exhibitions, while the fourth floor houses the **Politis Collection** which contains some fine ancient

What to Buy – Museum Replicas

Replica artefacts make fascinating souvenirs and they are often of a very high standard. Three museum shops renowned for their quality copies are the **National Archaeological Museum** (for statues and pottery), the **Benáki Museum** (for embroidery, jewellery and ceramics) and the **Goulandrís Museum of Cycladic Art** (for Cycladic figurines).

Below: *The Goulandrís Museum of Cycladic and Ancient Greek Art is famous for its Cycladic figurines.*

Learn Greek

The Athens Centre, 48 Arhimidous, tel: 210 701 2268, in the Athenian suburb of Mets, offers Greek language courses for beginners.

vases and bronze helmets. In 1992, the museum extended into the adjacent neoclassical **Stathátos Mansion** which currently houses the Greek art collection from the Athens Academy. There is a café in the courtyard between the two buildings, as well as a shop selling excellent replica Cycladic figurines. Located at 4 Neophytou Douka, open 10:00–16:00 Monday, Wednesday–Friday, 10:00–15:00 Saturday, closed Sunday and Tuesday.

Byzantine and Christian Museum ***

Recently expanded and modernized, the Byzantine and Christian Museum showcases icons, sculptures, mosaics, woodcarvings, manuscripts, frescoes, ecclesiastical robes and jewellery dating from the 4th–19th centuries. Occupying a graceful Florentine-style mansion that was home to the French Duchess de Plaisance in the mid-1800s, the museum was established in 1930. Two of the galleries are arranged as an Early Christian and Middle Byzantine chapel. Key exhibits include a 4th-century **funerary stele** showing Orpheus playing a lyre, a 7th-century **gold necklace** from the Mytilene treasure, and an 11th-century **marble slab** depicting three of the apostles. Among the stunning collection of **icons**, three of the most important are the 13th-century double-sided icon of *St George*, the 14th-century mosaic icon of the *Virgin and Child*, and the 18th-century icon of the *Virgin Nursing the Child*. Located at 22 Vasilíssis Sofías, open 08:30–15:00 Tuesday–Sunday.

Below: *This modern sculpture, entitled* The Runner, *can be seen near the National Gallery of Art.*

Museum of Greek Costume *

This specialist museum has a collection of traditional costumes gathered from different regions of Greece. Located at 7 Dimokritou, open 10:00–13:00 Monday, Wednesday and Friday.

Above: *Fighter jets outside the War Museum.*

National Gallery of Art **

A new wing was added to the National Gallery in 2000, while further hanging space is expected by 2004. There is a permanent European exhibition including five paintings by one of Greece's most renowned artists, **El Greco** (1541–1614). These include *Concert of Angels*, *St Peter* and *The Burial of Christ* which was bought in 2000 for US$700,000. Works by Brueghel, Cézanne, Goya, Picasso, Rembrandt and Van Dyck are also on display. The National Gallery is located at 50 Vasiléos Konstantínou, open 09:00–15:00 Monday and Wednesday–Saturday, 10:00–14:00 Sunday. Outside you can't miss the dynamic contemporary statue of ***The Runner*** by Kóstas Varotsos.

War Museum *

Difficult to miss with its display of fighter aircraft and military hardware outside the entrance, the War Museum traces battles, weaponry, armour, uniforms and strategies from Mycenaean times to World War II. Scale models depict battle scenes and fortified towns, such as Nafplio, while paintings and prints portray leaders from the War of Independence and evocative scenes from the two world wars. Corner of Vasilíssis Sofías and Rizári, open 09:00–14:00 Tuesday–Sunday.

GENNÁDEION

Home to a comprehensive library of over 70,000 books (including many rare first editions and illuminated manuscripts), the Gennádeion also contains nearly 200 sketches by Edward Lear and an eclectic display of Byron memorabilia. 61 Soudías, open 09:00–17:00 Mon–Tue and Fri, 09:00–20:00 Wed–Thu, 09:00–14:00 Sat.

Above: *Chic and sophisticated, Kolonáki has plenty of fashionable cafés and designer boutiques.*

Shopping and Eating Out

Kolonáki is abuzz with shoppers. Most of the city's top **designer boutiques** are located around Kolonáki Square or streets leading from it, while exclusive **jewellers** are concentrated on Voukourestiou (off Akadimías). You will also find **souvenir shops** near the funicular railway station at the top of Ploutarchou Street.

Trendy bars and places to eat also abound. This is the place to come if you want to pose at **outdoor cafés** with wealthy Athenians (or those pretending to be) – but don't forget your designer sunglasses.

Exárchia

With the exception of the not-to-be-missed **National Archaeological Museum**, this northern district of Central Athens lies off the main tourist track. It hit the world headlines on 17 November 1973 when many students were killed by the Junta during a protest (*see* page 16).

Exploring the Area

Along with the Acropolis and Ancient Agora, the National Archaeological Museum is one of the city's must-sees. Undergoing a major renovation in time for the 2004 Olympics, it houses the world's finest collection of Greek antiquities. Next door to the museum is the **Polytechnic**, from where it's a short stroll along Stournari Street to reach **Plateía Exarchéion** – a lively area lined with bars and cafés that are popular with students.

Nearby are the peaceful green havens of **Stréfi Hill** and **Areós Park**. The former has views of the Acropolis, while the latter is Athens' biggest park and contains wide tree-lined avenues and statues of heroes from the War of Independence. Several theatres are dotted around this area, as well as in the neighbouring districts of Vathi

On the Menu

Taramasaláta: pureed mullet roe and breadcrumbs.
Tzatzíki: yoghurt with cucumber, garlic and mint.
Melitzanosaláta: grilled aubergines and herbs.
Ntolmádes: vine leaves stuffed with rice, pine nuts and currants.
Saganáki: slices of cheese fried in olive oil.
Kotópoulo riganáto: spit-roasted chicken.
Arní me vótana: casserole of lamb on the bone with vegetables and herbs.
Psária plakí: whole fish baked in a vegetable and tomato sauce.
Kalamária: fried squid.
Giaoúrti kai méli: yoghurt with honey.

and Omónia. The **National Theatre** is just off **Plateía Omonías** (a traffic-clogged square that is being redeveloped to restore some of its former grandeur). Walk south from here down Athinas Street towards the Acropolis and you'll pass the **Town Hall** and **Central Market** before entering the district of Monastiráki.

National Archaeological Museum ***

Such is the importance of the collections in this world-class museum that, at the outbreak of World War II, they were dispersed and buried for safekeeping. Opened in 1891, the National Archaeological Museum with its neoclassical façade closed in 2002 for a major overhaul. It is due to reopen in April 2004.

The museum's priceless collections span the millennia, providing a comprehensive overview of Greek history and art. One of the earliest exhibits is a **Neolithic clay figurine** of a seated man, dated to 3200BC and found in Thessaly. The minimalist, contemporary-looking Cycladic style is represented by the **Harpist** (2800–2300BC) and a **folded-arm female figurine** from Amorgós which is the largest of its kind ever found.

Below: *Recently closed for major renovation, the National Archaeological Museum contains a priceless collection of artefacts.*

Key Periods

- Neolithic and Early Helladic 5000–2000BC
- Middle Helladic 2000–1600BC
- Late Helladic 1600–1100BC
- Dark Ages (Geometric) 1100–770BC
- Archaic 770–500BC
- Classical 500–323BC
- Hellenistic 323–30BC
- Roman 30BC–AD330
- Byzantine AD330–1452

Thíra frescoes discovered at Akrotíra on Santoríni in 1967 and dating from 1500BC are also on display. The star exhibit from this period, however, is undoubtedly the stunning collection of **Mycenaean gold** and other artefacts excavated from the grave shafts at Ancient Mycenae (*see* page 117). The most famous piece is the **Mask of Agamemnon** – a gold death mask dating from the latter half of the 16th century BC thought by its discoverer, Schliemann, to have belonged to the legendary king, Agamemnon. Other Mycenaean treasures include a **bronze dagger** inlaid with gold and depicting a lion-hunting scene, and the gold **Vafeió Cups** that were discovered in a tholos (beehive-shaped tomb) on Crete. There are also Linear B tablets, gold seals and a boar's tusk helmet.

Following the demise of the Mycenaean civilization around 1150BC, the museum picks up the trail of Greek art revival with some magnificent vases from the late Geometric period. Particularly striking is a **funerary amphora** from the 8th century BC that was found near the Dípylon Gate at Kerameikós (*see* page 43). An early **black-figure vase** (ca.620BC) depicting Heracles killing the Centaur can also be seen.

Archaic sculpture dating from around the 7th century BC includes the **Soúnion *Kouros*** – a colossal votive statue measuring over 3m (10ft) in height that was found in the Temple of Poseidon at Cape Soúnion (*see* page 88). Other Archaic beauties not to be missed are the **Phrasikleia *Kore*** and **Aristodikos *Kouros*** with their serene smiles and relaxed poses, as well as the earliest known Nike (or winged goddess of victory) dated to 550BC.

Among the exhibits of classical sculpture are some beautifully carved funerary **stelae** from Kerameikós (including the **Stele of Hegeso** from the early 5th century BC) and a reduced copy of the original gold and ivory **statue of Athena** from the Parthenon.

Some of the museum's most memorable exhibits are of sculptures from the Hellenistic era. Raised from a shipwreck off Cape Artemísion on the island of Évia, the enigmatic bronzes of ***Poseidon*** and the ***Jockey*** have been dated to ca.460BC and ca.140BC respectively. Other magnificent finds, dated to around 340BC, include the ***Youth of Antikythira***, a statue of a god or hero standing 2m (7ft) tall that was also found in an ancient shipwreck, and the ***Marathon Boy***, a wonderfully poised figure from the school of Praxiteles – one of the leading late classical sculptors. Another masterpiece well worth looking out for is the marble group of ***Aphrodite***, ***Pan*** and ***Eros*** from the 2nd century BC that was found on Deros. The goddess is shown raising her sandal to ward off an over-attentive goat-footed Pan. Also not to be missed is the exquisite **Ilissos Stele** showing an Ethiopian groom with his horse.

Above: *According to Greek mythology, Zeus, depicted in this sculpture at the National Archaeological Museum, was the supreme ruler of Mount Olympus and the Pantheon of gods which resided there.*

Opposite: *This Herculean woman, dating from the Roman period, is one of many fine statues on display at the National Archaeological Museum.*

The Roman period is represented by busts of key figures, such as Hadrian, as well as a bronze statue of Augustus dredged from the Aegean.

Other collections at the museum are dedicated to pottery, bronzes, Egyptian art and jewellery. Highlights from these include **white-ground *lekythos* vases** from the 5th century BC, a bronze of a **Boiotian warrior** from the 7th century BC, part of a **statue of a pharaoh** (ca.2500 BC) and the famous gold jewellery and *objets d'art* of the **Stathátos Collection** covering the Bronze Age through to the Byzantine period.

The National Archaeological Museum is located at 44 Patissíon, open 12:30–19:00 Monday, 08:00–19:00 Tuesday–Friday, 08:30–15:00 Saturday–Sunday, April to mid-October; 11:00–17:00 Monday, 08:00–17:00 Tuesday–Friday, 08:00–15:00 Saturday and Sunday, mid-October to March.

Sharing the same building, but accessed via 1 Tositsa Street, is the **Epigraphic Museum** (open 08:30–14:30 Tuesday–Sunday) which contains stone inscriptions ranging from tribute lists to the decree of Themistocles in 480BC ordering the evacuation of Athens before the Persian invasion.

Above: *The Olympic Stadium is part of the Athens Olympic Sports Complex in Maroussi, a northern suburb of Athens 9km (6 miles) from city centre and 22km (14 miles) from the international airport. It is one of many sporting venues that will be 'upgraded' for the 2004 Olympic Games.*

The Northern Suburbs

Hemmed in by hills to the east and west and the Saronic Gulf to the south, modern Athens has little alternative but to spread northwards. The metro is probably the quickest way to reach the city's northern suburbs. Stop at Irini for the **Olympic Stadium**, at Maroússi for the **Spathári Shadow Theatre Museum** and at Kifissiá for the **Goulandrís Natural History Museum**. Kifissiá, a leafy suburb favoured by the wealthy ever since Herodes Atticus had a villa built here, can be explored in one of the horse-drawn carriages waiting by the metro station. Nearby is **Mount Pendéli**, site of a monastery founded in 1578, as well as the **ancient quarries** from which the famous Pentelic marble was cut for the Parthenon.

Olympic Stadium ★

Originally built in 1982 for the 1996 Olympic games (that went to Atlanta), the 78,000-seat Olympic Stadium has been biding its time as Athens' premier soccer venue until it takes centre stage for the 2004 Olympics. Revamped with state-of-the-art touches, such as temperature-regulating ponds and a special roof designed to admit light but not heat, the Olympic Stadium will stage the athletics events, as well as the opening and closing ceremonies. Nearby, as part of the Olympic Sports Complex, are additional facilities for swimming, gymnastics, basketball, cycling, tennis and water polo.

Agamemnon (Greek Legend)

Background: King of Mycenae.
Achievements: leading the Greeks at the siege of Troy (according to Homer's *Iliad*).
Best known for: his gold funerary mask uncovered at Ancient Mycenae by the archaeologist, Schliemann, in the mid-1800s (despite modern dating techniques suggesting it belongs to an earlier king).

Spathári Shadow Theatre Museum ★

This quirky museum reveals the fascinating history of shadow puppet theatre – a popular folk art that has its roots in the Far East. Located at 22 Argonáfton, Maroússi, open 10:00–13:30 Monday–Friday.

Goulandrís Natural History Museum ★

Showcasing an extensive collection of plants, animals and minerals from Greece and further afield, this award-winning museum (opened in 1975) is located in one of Kifissiá's large villas. Located at 13 Levídou, open 09:00–14:30 Saturday–Thursday.

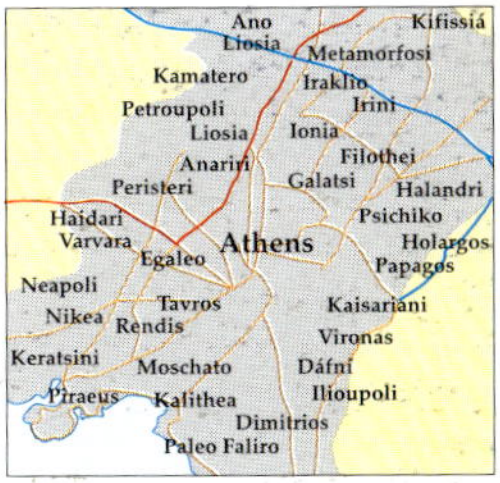

The Railway Museum

Located at 301 Liossion Street, in the Athenian suburb of Sepolia, the Railway Museum (open 09:00–13:00 Mon–Fri, 17:00–20:00 Wed, 09:00–13:00 Sun) contains a collection of old city trams, an 1899 steam locomotive and a carriage from the rack railway of Diakofto-Kalavrita.

Solon (early 6th century BC)

Background: Athenian statesman and poet.
Achievements: introducing revolutionary economic, political and social reforms.
Best known for: laying the foundations of democracy in ancient Athens.

Left: *Olympic swimming pool, one of the venues for the 2004 Games.*

Athens at a Glance

Best Times To Visit

Spring and autumn are the best times to visit. Not only is it pleasantly warm and sunny, but the city's main sites and museums will be less crowded. Even as late as November the temperature can be a comfortable 23°C (73°F), while January, the coldest month, usually only drops to a minimum of 12°C (54°F). Winter months, however, are also the wettest (snow is not unheard of). By contrast, summer (June–September) is usually dry with daytime temperatures reaching uncomfortable highs. This is also the most expensive and crowded time to visit.

Getting There

By air: The national carrier, Olympic Airways (96 Syngroú, tel: 210 966 6666, www.olympic-airways.gr), operates flights between Athens and a range of worldwide locations, including Australia, Canada, Cyprus, Turkey and the UK. British Airways (1 Themistokléos, Glyfáda, tel: 210 890 6666, www.ba.com) has flights from Heathrow, Gatwick and Birmingham to Athens, while KLM (41 Vouliagménis, Glyfáda, tel: 210 960 5010) and Air France (18 Vouliagménis, Glyfáda, tel: 210 960 1100) fly from Amsterdam and Paris respectively. *See* Travel Tips, pages 122–123 for a full list of airlines in Athens.

International flights arrive at the modern **Elefthérios Venizélos International Airport**, located 21km (13 miles) northeast of Athens city centre. The airport has shops, restaurants, banks, car hire and tourist information. There is a charge for trolleys – change machines are available in the baggage hall. A useful transit hotel, the Sofitel (*see* page 73), is nearby.

Airport buses connect with the metro at Ethniki Amina, Metro line 3 (green line). The E95 24hr airport bus operates every 10–30min to Syntagma, stopping outside the National Gardens on Amalías. The journey takes around 50min depending on traffic. Purchase a ticket (¤2.95) at the nearby kiosk. Once validated (by inserting it into the machine on the bus as soon as you board) the ticket allows for unlimited travel by all public transport modes over the following 24hr period. Children under six travel free. Taxis are always available at the airport (expect to pay around €20 for a downtown destination – more after midnight). If you are collecting a hire car at the airport, don't set off for the city without some small change (€0.60) – part of the route is along a toll road.

By road: Long-distance buses, such as Eurolines (www.eurolines.com) connect Athens with the rest of Europe. Buses from destinations within Greece arrive and depart from one of four stations: **Terminal A** (100 Kifissoú St) for Argos, Corinth, Kalamata, Nafplio, Olympia, Pátras and Tripoli, and **Terminal B** (Agiou Dimitriou Oplon) for Delphi, Évia, Volos and Meteora; **Mavromateon Terminal** (28 Oktovriou-Patisson) for eastern Attica and the port of Rafína, and **Thissio Terminal** (near the metro station) for Elefsína, Megara and Porto Germano.

By rail: International trains arrive via Thessaloníki at Athens' Larissa Station, on Deliyiánni Street. Eurostar (www.eurostar.com) operates trains from the UK to Paris or Brussels with onward connections to Athens. There are also services from northern Greece and the Peloponnese. For details of services, contact OSE, 1–3 Karolou, tel: 210 522 2491, www.ose.gr

By sea: Ferries from Crete, the Cyclades, the Dodecanese and the Saronic islands serve the port at Piraeus, near Athens.

Packages: In the UK, the following travel agents offer city breaks in Athens: Travelscene, tel: 020 8424 9648, www.travelscene.co.uk Cresta, tel: 0161 385 4100, www.crestaholidays.co.uk and Sunvil, tel: 020 8568 4499, www.sunvil.co.uk

Getting Around

Once you are in the Syntagma-Pláka area, you will probably have little need

Athens at a Glance

of public transport since most sites and museums are within easy walking distance. For longer journeys, however, the modern and efficient metro is ideal. There are also buses, trolleys and taxis – but these are all at the mercy of traffic jams. Pick up a free copy of the *Athens Public Transport Pocket Map* which marks the main metro, bus and trolley routes.

By metro: The three lines of the Athens Metro converge at the city centre with main intersections at Syntagma, Monastiráki, Attiki and Omónia. **Line 1 (green)** operates between Kifissiá in the north and Piraeus in the south, with useful stops at Irini (for the Olympic stadium), Victoria (for the National Archaeological Museum) and Monastiráki (for several main sites, including the Ancient Agora). **Line 2 (red)** runs between Sepolia in the northwest and Dáfní in the southeast and includes stops at Larissa (for train stations), Syntagma (for the Parliament building and National Gardens) and Akropoli (for the Acropolis). **Line 3 (blue)** links Ethniki Amyna in the east with Monastiráki and has stops for Evangelismos (for museums in Kolonáki) and Syntagma. Lines 2 and 3 are ungergoing extensions to bring outlying residential and business areas within the metro network.

Athens Metro operates daily 05:00–24:00, running every 3–10min. A standard ticket costs €0.75, although it is worth considering purchasing a day ticket for €3 which

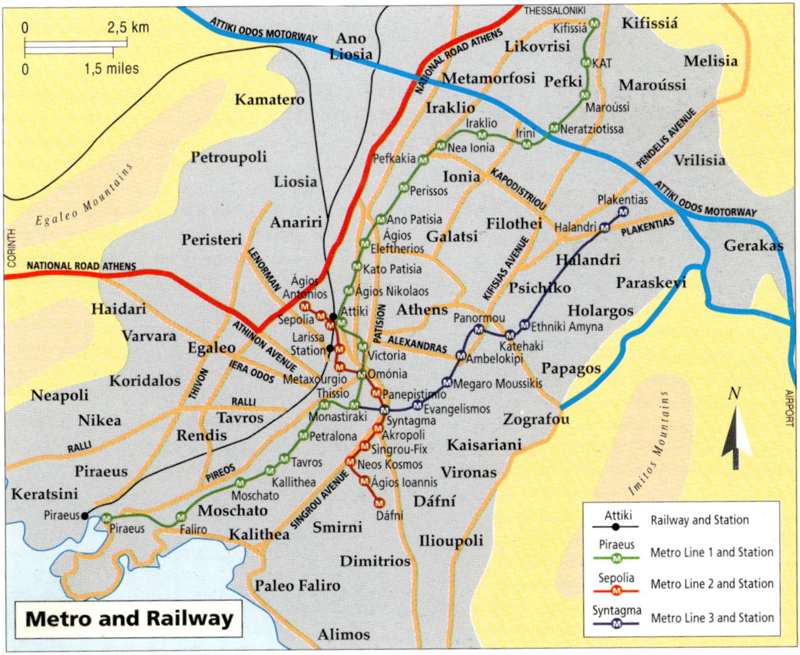

Metro and Railway

Athens at a Glance

allows travel on all city transport for 24hr.
By bus and trolley: Operating from 05:00–24:00, trolleys and buses have a flat fare of around €0.50 for all city routes. Purchase tickets at the yellow and blue kiosks located near terminals and validate them using the red machines as soon as you board. There is a spot fine for travelling with a non-validated ticket. Bus lines are coloured differently depending on direction of travel: orange (central lines), blue (southerly), red (northerly), brown (westerly) and green (easterly).
By taxi: Although there are a few official stands, most taxis simply cruise the streets. That means you have to stand by the curb, flag down any passing taxi and (assuming the cabbie shows any interest by slowing down) shout out where you want to go. The best place to find a taxi is usually outside one of the big hotels. Taxis are often shared, so if your destination roughly fits in with where the driver is heading, you may be in luck. Meters do not always work, so establish an approximate rate before setting off. If your journey is urgent, book a radio taxi: Athina, tel: 210 921 7942, Enotita, tel: 210 645 9000 or Parthenon, tel: 210 581 4711.
Car rental: Driving yourself around Athens is not recommended. Apart from traffic jams, the city has a perplexing one-way system and scant parking. Besides, your feet and the metro will get you places far quicker than driving. *See* Travel Tips, page 124 for car rental companies.

Where to Stay

Athens stays up late, so if your hotel is on a busy, noisy street, it may be worth requesting a room at the rear – even if you forsake the view. Pláka, close to many of the city's top sites and offering a wide range of accommodation styles and price categories, is the most popular place to stay – book well in advance, particularly during the high season. If you are having trouble finding a room, try the **Hotel Association**, Syntagma Square, tel: 210 323 7193, open 08:30–14:00 Mon–Thu, 08:30–13:00 Fri, 09:00–13:00 Sat.

Luxury

Andromeda, 22 Timoléontos Vássou, Ampelokipoi, tel: 210 641 5000, www.andromedaathens.gr This immaculate boutique-style hotel is a member of the Small Luxury Hotels of the World and is located in a quiet street behind the concert hall.
Athenaeum Inter-Continental, 89–93 Syngroú, Neos Kosmos, tel: 210 920 6000, www.inter-continental.com A modern hotel with spacious rooms, a health club, pool and rooftop restaurant offering lovely views towards the Acropolis.
Athenian Inn, 22 Cháritos, Kolonáki, tel: 210 723 8097. In the heart of Kolonáki's shopping and dining district.
Divanis Caravel, 2 Vassiléos Alexándrou, Kaisarianí, tel: 210 720 7000, www.divanicaravel.gr Located close to the National Gallery, with spacious rooms, a heated outdoor pool and roof garden.
Divani Palace Acropolis, 19–25 Parthenónos, Makrigiánni, tel: 210 928 0100, www.divaniacropolis.gr Close to Pláka and the Acropolis, this stylish hotel displays a section of the ancient Themistoclean Long Walls in its lobby.
Electra Palace, 18 Nikodímou, Pláka, tel: 210 337 0000. Offering views of Acropolis, the Electra has good facilities including a garage and rooftop pool.
Grande Bretagne, Syntagma Square, tel: 210 333 0000, www.starwood.com A city landmark, this former royal palace was built in 1862 and was used as a Nazi headquarters, then by Winston Churchill. Modernized in 2002, it offers superb style and service with a beautiful marble lobby and luxurious rooms.
Holiday Inn, 50 Mihalokopoúlou, Ilisia, tel: 210 727 8000, www.hiathensgreece.com Modern hotel with comfortable rooms and a rooftop pool.

Athens at a Glance

Hilton, 46 Leofóros Vasilíssis Sofías, Ilisia, tel: 210 728 1000, www.hilton.com Extensively renovated in 2003, the Hilton boasts superb facilities and stunning city views.
Ledra Marriott, 113–115 Syngroú, Neos Kosmos, tel: 210 930 0000, www.marriott.com All the comforts and amenities of a modern luxury hotel with large rooms, excellent restaurants and a hydrotherapy centre.
Pentelikón, 66 Diligiánni Street, Kifissiá, tel: 210 623 06507. A fine hotel with beautiful rooms, a Michelin-starred restaurant, a garden and pool; close to the metro station.
Royal Olympic, 28–32 Diákou, Makrigiánni, tel: 010 922 6411. Great views of the Temple of Olympian Zeus, plus large rooms, a rooftop bar and excellent grill restaurant.
Sofitel, opposite Athens International Airport; tel: 210 354 4000, fax: 210 354 4444, www.sofitel.com Convenient hotel with two restaurants, a bar and a fitness centre with indoor swimming pool.
St George Lycabettus, 2 Kleoménous, Kolonáki, tel: 210 729 0711, www.sglycabettus.gr On the slopes of Lykavitós Hill, this hotel has stunning views, as well as large, modern rooms and a wonderful art collection.

Mid-range

Achilleas, 21 Leka, Pláka, tel: 210 323 3197. The top-floor rooms open on to a garden terrace.
Acropolis House, 6–8 Kódrou, Pláka, tel: 210 322 3244. Large rooms in a wonderful old pension with antique furnishings, high ceilings and balconies.
Adonis, 3 Kódrou, Pláka, tel: 210 324 9737. Modern hotel with roof garden and rooms with balconies and views.
Amalia, 10 Amalías, Syntagma, tel: 210 323 7301, www.amalia.gr Clean, basic rooms and a great location opposite the National Gardens.
Aphrodite, 21 Apóllonos, Pláka, tel: 210 323 4357. Good location with some rooms offering views of the Acropolis.
Astor, 16 Karagiórgi Servías, Syntagma, tel: 210 335 1000. Excellent central location and stunning views from rooftop restaurant.
Cecil, 39 Athinas, Monastiráki, tel: 210 321 7909. Recently refurbished, with high ceilings, timber floors and well-equipped rooms.
Ermís, 19 Apóllonos, Pláka, tel: 210 323 5514. Large rooms and roof garden.
Kouros, 11 Kódrou, Pláka, tel: 210 322 7431. Great location in the heart of Pláka, clean basic rooms in a converted neoclassical mansion.
Iródeion, 4 Rovértou Gkálli, Makrigiánni, tel: 210 923 6832. Located close to Herodes Atticus Theatre, modern, comfortable rooms and a patio shaded by pistachio trees.
Nefeli, 16 Iperidou, Pláka, tel: 210 322 8044. Quiet location with comfortable rooms.
Parthenon, 6 Makrí, Makrigiánni, tel: 210 923 4594. Close to Akropoli metro, clean comfortable rooms, some with views.
Titánia, 52 Panepistimíou, Omónia tel: 210 330 0111, www.titania.gr A popular rooftop restaurant (the Olive Garden), plus good views, well-equipped rooms and parking.

Budget

Faidrá, 16 Chairefóntos, Pláka, tel: 210 323 8461. Located near Lysikrátous Monument, basic rooms.
John's Place, 5 Patróou, Pláka, tel: 210 322 9719. Small, clean rooms with shared bathrooms. Ideal location.
Marble House, 35 Anastasiou Zinni, Koukáki, tel: 210 923 4058. Pension with mostly *en-suite* rooms.
Museum, 16 Mpoumpoulínas, Exárchia, tel: 210 380 5611. Located behind the National Archaeological Museum, clean modern rooms with *en-suite* bathrooms.
Témpi, 29 Eólou, Monastiráki, tel: 210 321 3175. Good location near the metro station, a friendly and clean hotel popular with students.

Athens at a Glance

Where to Eat

Athenians rarely dine before 22:00 and many restaurant opening times reflect this. Try the Pláka area for the best range of traditional tavernas – many opening earlier in the evening to cater to tourists. Some of the top restaurants close down in summer and move to sister properties in the islands.

Luxury

Aigli Bistrot, Záppeion Gardens, tel: 210 336 9363. Mediterranean-style food served in a great location with outdoor jazz and cinema in summer.
Beau Brummel, 19 Agiou Dimitriou, Kifissiá, tel: 210 623 6780. Internationally acclaimed French restaurant.
Boschetto, Evangelismos Park, Kolonáki, tel: 210 721 0893. Fine Italian food in a garden setting. Excellent wine selection.
Dáfni, 4 Lysikrátous, Pláka, tel: 210 322 7971. A converted neoclassical mansion makes this a great venue for modern Greek dishes, with specialities like swordfish and pork meatballs.
Edodi, 80 Veikou, Koukáki, tel: 210 921 3013. Small, stylish restaurant in a neoclassical mansion. Exciting *haute cuisine* and impeccable service.
GB Corner, Grande Bretagne Hotel, Syntagma, tel: 210 333 0000. Renowned for excellent service, this quality restaurant serves Greek and international food.
Ideal, 46 Panepistimíou, Omónia, tel: 210 330 3000. Established in 1922. A tasty and varied range of Greek and international cuisine with many specialities.
Interni, 152 Ermoú, Gazi, tel: 210 346 8900. Designer restaurant serving Italian-Asian fusion cuisine.
Kiku, 12 Dimokrítou, Kolonáki, tel: 210 364 7033. The place in Athens to eat Japanese sushi. Pricey but stylish.
Pil Poule, 51 Apostólou Pávlou, Thissio, tel: 210 342 3665. Classy restaurant with stunning Acropolis views and fine wine list. Trendy Mediterranean dishes with strong French influence.
Spondí, 5 Pyrronos, Pangrati, tel: 210 756 4021. Greek food with a modern twist, extensive wine list and fine desserts. Lovely neoclassical mansion with courtyard for summer dining.
Symposio, 46 Herodeio, Makrigiánni, tel: 210 922 5321. Delicious modern Greek food served in the garden or conservatory of a neoclassical mansion. Try the signature dish of fish baked in a salt crust.

Mid-range

Cellier Le Bistrot, 10 Panepistimíou, Syntagma, tel: 210 363 8535. Extensive wine list and a good range of light meals make this a good lunch venue.
Eden, 12 Lysíou, Pláka, tel: 210 324 8858. Long-established vegetarian restaurant using organic produce.
Kallimármaron, 13 Eforionos, Pangrati, tel: 210 701 9727. Located near the old Olympic stadium, this family-run taverna serves traditional Greek dishes.
Nefeli, 24 Panos, Pláka, tel: 210 321 2475. Taverna and coffee shop next to the Ancient Agora, serving lunch and dinner.
O Mpókaris, 17 Sokrátous, Kifissiá, tel: 210 801 2589. Renowned taverna with excellent grills and pies.
Platanos, 4 Diogénis, Pláka, tel: 210 322 0666. Long-established taverna near Lysikrátous Monument.
Stavlos, 10 Irakleidon, Thissio, tel: 210 346 7206. Situated in old Royal Stables. Bar and restaurant with art gallery.
Terína, 25 Kapnikaréas, Pláka, tel: 210 321 5015. Lovely location in Agorás Square, good taverna food.
Zidoron, 10 Táki, Psirrí, tel: 210 321 5368. Popular eatery renowned for its delicious *mezédes*.

Budget

Athinaikón, 2 Themistokléous, Omónia, tel: 210 383 8485. Long-established and popular restaurant with lots of atmos-

Athens at a Glance

phere and a good menu of *mezédes* and seafood dishes.

Diporto, 9 Sokrátous, Monastiráki, tel: 210 321 1463. Basement taverna serving simple and delicious traditional fare.

Ouzeri Kouklis, 14 Tripodon, Pláka, tel: 210 324 7605. An old favourite of locals and tourists alike. *Mezédes*, wine and ouzo.

Strofi, 25 Rovertou Gkalli, Acropolis, tel: 210 921 4130. Stunning rooftop views guarantee the popularity of this traditional taverna.

Taki 13, 13 Taki, Psirrí, tel: 210 325 4707. Great atmosphere with live music. Simple, but tasty range of *mezédes*.

Taverna Barbargiannis, 94 Emmanual Benáki, Exárchia, tel: 210 330 0185. Delicious daily specials are chalked up on the blackboard inside this popular taverna.

Taverna tou Psirrí, 12 Aischylou, Psirrí, tel: 210 321 4923. Hearty Greek cuisine with dishes taking their inspiration from the owner's home island of Náxos.

Taverna Vicantino, 18 Kydathineon, Pláka, tel: 210 322 7368. Popular with locals, this taverna serves all the traditional favourites.

Thanasis, 69 Mitropóleos, Monastiráki, tel: 210 324 4705. Excellent souvlakia to take away or eat in.

To Steki tou Elia, 5 Epahalkou, Thissio, tel: 210 345 8052. Renowned for lamb chops, but also serves excellent steaks and salads.

Cafés

Kolonáki Square has a reputation for the best coffee in Athens, but there are also plenty of cafés throughout the city offering everything from strong Greek coffee to ice cream and traditional pastries and sweets.

Brazil Coffee Shop, 1 Voukourestiou, Syntagma, tel: 210 323 5463. Range of coffees, plus cakes and pastries.

Dodoni, 9 Milioni, Kolonáki, tel: 210 363 7387. Ice cream galore.

Filion, 34 Skoufa, Kolonáki, tel: 210 361 2850. Copious cakes.

Kotsolis, 112 Adrianoú, Pláka, tel: 210 322 1164. Traditional sweets and pastries.

To Tistrato, corner of Aggelou Geronta and Dedalou, Pláka, tel: 210 324 4472. Tea, coffee and desserts.

Varsos, 5 Kassaveti, Kifissiá, tel: 210 801 3743. Historic patisserie dating back to 1892. Mouth-watering range of sweets and pastries, plus excellent coffee.

Entertainment

Athens boasts an exciting range of bars, clubs, music and dance venues, festivals and theatre. English-language listings can be found in the daily *Kathimerini* supplement (in the *International Herald Tribune*), the weekly *Athens News* and the quarterly *Welcome to Athens* (available from the tourist office).

Bars and clubs: The districts of Psirrí, Kolonáki and Gazi are the places to go for serious nightlife. However, you will find venues scattered across the capital, ranging from mellow bars to pounding nightclubs. Some only operate between October and April, moving to the coast during summer.

Banana Moon, next to the old Olympic Stadium, Mets, tel: 210 752 1768. A trendy bar and disco.

Bedlam, in the Záppeion Gardens, Syntagma, tel: 210 336 9340. A 'cool' new summer bar.

Brettos, 41 Kydathineon, Pláka, tel: 210 323 2110. An old-fashioned bar lined with wine barrels and bottles.

Inoteka, Plateía Avyssinnías, Monastiráki, tel: 210 324 6446. A low-key candlelit bar.

Stavlos, 10 Iraklidon, Thissio, tel: 210 346 7206. A lively bar with rock music.

Thirio, 2 Lepenioutou, Psirrí, tel: 210 722 4104. A happening, often crowded club with loud music.

For **Rembetika clubs**, playing the so-called Greek blues, head for **Stoa Athanaton**, 19 Sofokleous, Omónia,

Athens at a Glance

tel: 210 321 4362. The gay scene in Athens is centred on the district of Makrigiánni where one of the most popular clubs is **Lamda**, 15 Lembesi, tel: 210 942 4202.

Cinemas: Mainstream cinemas in Athens showing films with Greek subtitles include the **Apollon & Attikon Renault**, 19 Stadíou, tel: 210 323 6811, the **Elly**, 64 Akadimías, tel: 210 363 2789, and the **Ideal**, 46 Panepistimíou, tel: 210 382 6720. The annual **Athens Film Festival** (tel: 210 606 1413, www.aiff.gr) takes place in September at the Apollon & Attikon Renault. Watching a film at an **outdoor cinema** is a wonderful way to spend a summer evening. Some of the most popular venues are **Cine Pari**, a rooftop cinema at 22 Kydathineon, Pláka, tel: 210 322 2071; **Aigli** in the Záppeion Gardens, Syntagma, tel: 210 336 9369; **Dexameni** on Lykavitós Hill, Kolonáki, tel: 210 360 2363; and **Thisseion** at 7 Apostolou Pavlou, Thissio, tel: 210 342 0864.

Concerts: Boasting superb acoustics, the state-of-the-art **Mègaron Musikís** concert hall on Vasilissis Sofias, tel: 210 728 2333, features a range of classical performances, from opera to classical concerts – Greek and international. The **Greek National Opera**, 59 Akadimías, tel: 210 361 2461, hosts performances at the Olympia Theatre from November–June.

Festivals: From June–September, the **Theatre of Herodes Atticus** on the southern slope of the Acropolis is the magnificent historical venue for the Hellenic Festival (or **Festival of Athens**) – a showcase for classical and contemporary musicians, actors and dancers from around the world. Programme information and tickets are available from the Hellenic Festival box office, 4 Stadíou, tel: 210 322 1459, www.greekfestival.gr

Folk dance: The internationally-acclaimed Dóra Strátou traditional folk dance troupe perform every night (starting 21:30) from May–September at the **Dóra Strátou Dance Theatre** on Philopáppou Hill, tel: 210 921 4650.

Son et Lumière: A popular tourist activity, the sound and light show is held nightly (starting 21:00) in English at the **Hill of the Pnyx Theatre**, off Dionysiou Areópagitou, tel: 210 322 1459. During the show, music and narration accompany a mesmerizing play of light across the monuments of the Acropolis.

Shopping

Athens is a shopper's paradise. You can buy virtually anything – from a plastic, glow-in-the-dark Parthenon to an exquisite piece of designer jewellery. The focus for retail therapy is Ermoú Street – particularly if you are on the lookout for a new pair of shoes. Designer fashion victims should head for the boutiques in Kolonáki, Kifissiá and Maroússi. Elite jewellers are strung along Voukourestiou, off Akadimías, while sacks of olives, spices and nuts can be found at the Central Market. For souvenirs, your best bet is Pláka or Monastiráki. Greek music is in good supply at the Virgin Megastore, 7 Stadíou, Syntagma, and Metropolis, 64 Panepistimíou, Omónia, while English-language books can be found at Eleftheroudakis, 17 Panepistimíou. If a newspaper is all you are after, check out one of the many *periptera* (kiosks) dotted around the city. Some of the shopping highlights in Athens include:

Benáki Museum Gift Shop, 1 Koumbari, Kolonáki, tel: 210 362 7367. Great range of books, plus some tempting replicas of ancient artefacts.

Cellier, 1 Kriezotou, Syntagma, tel: 210 361 0040. Good range of Greek wines and liquers.

Central Market, Athinas, Omónia, open 07:00–15:00

Athens at a Glance

Mon–Sat. Feast your eyes on a bewildering array of meat, seafood, olives, spices, fruit and vegetables.
Centre of Hellenic Tradition, 36 Pandrosou, Monastiráki, tel: 210 321 3023. Excellent selection of traditional handicrafts, including carvings and paintings.
Christakis, 5 Kriezotou, Syntagma, tel: 210 361 3030. Well-known and exclusive tailor shop. Choose from dozens of rolls of fabric for that special handmade shirt.
Flea Market, centred on Plateía Avyssinías, Monastiráki, open 07:00–15:00 Sun (plus a number of permanent stores). A bargain-hunter's paradise where you'll find everything from kitsch to kitchen sinks. Antiques, collectables and furniture feature strongly.
Hellenic Folk Art Gallery, corner of Apollonos and Ipatias, Pláka, tel: 210 325 0524. Broad range of traditional handicrafts with proceeds going to the National Welfare Organization.
Ilias Lalaounis, 6 Panepistimíou, Kolonáki, tel: 210 361 1371. World-renowned jewellers creating exquisite pieces inspired by Greek and other cultures.
Martinos, 50 Pandrosou, Monastiráki, tel: 210 321 2414. Antiques from Greece and further afield, including icons, glassware and furniture.
Miseyiannis, 7 Leventi, Kolonáki, tel: 210 721 0136. Greek coffee and everything you need to make that authentic brew.
Museum of Cycladic Art Shop, 4 Neofitou Douka, Kolonáki, tel: 210 724 9706. Stunning range of replica Cycladic figurines.
Spiliopoulos, 63 Ermoú, Syntagma, tel: 210 322 7590. Shoes galore with plenty of top brands, often at bargain prices.
Stavros Melissinos, 89 Pandrosou, Monastiráki, tel: 210 321 9247. The famous poet and sandal maker of Athens.
Thiamis, 12 Apollonos, Pláka, tel: 210 331 0337. Beautiful, hand-painted icons. Your patron saint can be painted to order.
Zolotas, 9 Stadíou, Syntagma, tel: 210 331 3320. Internationally acclaimed jewellers specializing in replicas of ancient Greek museum pieces.

Sport

Golf and **tennis** facilities can be found at Glyfáda Golf Club, *see* page 93, while **ten-pin bowling** is available at the Athens Bowling Centre, 177 Oktovriou-Patission, tel: 210 867 3645. For **swimming**, your best option is a hotel pool or the beaches at the resorts south of Athens. For information on **spectator sports**, such as soccer, basketball, athletics and horse racing, visit the website of the Greek Secretariat for Sport (www.sport.gov.gr) which has details of all venues.

Tours and Excursions

The most popular half-day tours from Athens are **Athens Sightseeing** (a coach tour pointing out the major sites with stops at the Acropolis and the Temple of Olympian Zeus), **Athens by Night** (the son et lumière, followed by a meal at a taverna with folk dancing), **Cape Soúnion** (usually an afternoon coach tour to the site of the famous Temple of Poseidon, *see* page 88) and **Ancient Corinth** (a whistle-stop tour of the canal and archaelogical site, *see* page 116).
Full-day tours (and longer) are available to **Ancient Mycenae** (*see* page 117), **Epidaurus** (*see* page 118), **Ancient Olympia** (*see* page 119) and **Delphi** (*see* page 104), as well as cruises to the **Saronic Gulf islands** (*see* page 109).
Hotel reception areas and the tourist office are good places to pick up brochures advertising any of the above. Major tour companies in Athens include **CHAT**, 9 Xenofontos, tel: 210 322 3137, **GO Tours**, 20 Athanassiou, tel: 210 921 9555, and **Key Tours**, 4 Kalirois, tel: 210 923 3166.
Hop-In Sightseeing, 29 Zanni, Piraeus, tel: 210 428 5500, www.hopin.com

Athens at a Glance

operates buses on set routes which you can join or leave at various stops. There are longer stops at the Acropolis and National Archaeological Museum.

Ideal for families with young children (and big kids too), the **Fun Train** operates daily during the summer, 11:00–19:00, linking all the main sites between Syntagma and the Acropolis.

The **City of Athens**, tel: 210 323 1841, hosts free walking tours of the city's main sites every Sunday and second Saturday of the month, commencing 10:30. The **Panhellenic Guides Federation**, tel: 210 322 9705, can organize private tours to selected archaeological sites around the city. **Rania Vassiliadou**, tel: 210 940 3932, also provides a guiding service.

Useful Contacts

Tourist Information, Hellenic Tourism Organisation (EOT), 2 Amerikis St, close to Syntagma Square, tel: 210 331 0561, www, gnto.gr open 09:00–16:00 Mon–Fri, 10:00–15:00 Sat. The EOT produces a booklet, *Greece: Athens*, as well as information on a variety of useful topics, such as ferry departures from Piraeus and Athens public transport. A free map of central Athens is also available. The EOT also have an office at the international airport, tel: 210 353 0445, open 08:00–22:00 daily.

For accommodation, flights, ferries, etc., try www.gtp.net

Tourist Police, tel: 171, from 07:00–23:00 daily, answer (in English) tourist queries and assist with any emergencies.

Police, tel: 100.

Ambulance, tel: 166.

Emergency hospitals tel: 106.

Hospitals: Evangelismos (public), 45–47 Ipsilantou, Kolonáki, tel: 210 720 1000; **Athens Euroclinic** (private), 9 Athanasiadou, Ambelokipi, tel: 210 641 6600.

Fire brigade tel: 199.

Currency exchange: National Bank of Greece, Syntagma Square, 08:00–14:00 and 15:30–17:30 Mon–Fri, 09:00–15:00 Sat, 09:00–13:00 Sun. There are also banks at the international airport, open 07:00–21:00.

Airport information, tel: 210 353 0000, 24hr a day for flight information available in both Greek and English.

Left luggage: Pacific Travel, 26 Nikis, Pláka, tel: 210 324 1007, and also at the airport near gate 1 on Arrivals, tel: 210 353 0160.

Post Offices: Syntagma Square and 100 Eolou, Omónia. Both are open 07:30–20:00 Mon–Fri, 07:30–14:00 Sat, 09:00–13:00 Sun.

Email and Internet: Astor Internet Café, 27 Oktovriou-Patission, Omónia, open 10:00–22:00 daily; **Pláka Internet World**, 29 Pandrosou, Monastiráki, open 11:00–23:00 daily; **Sofokleous.com Internet Café**, 5 Stadíou, Syntagma, 10:00–22:00 Mon–Sat, 13:00–21:00 Sun.

City Walks

The following walks provide an excellent introduction to many of the highlights of Athens. Although they have been devised to last a whole day and take into account the early closing times of many archaeological sites, you should check in advance when certain museums and archaeological sites are open.

Acropolis Circuit

Start/end: Akropoli Metro

1. Turn left into pedestrianized Dionysiou Areopagitou and walk past the ancient theatres of Dionysos and Herodes Atticus.
2. Take the path leading to the Acropolis and spend the morning exploring the Parthenon and other highlights.
3. Leaving the Acropolis, turn right along Thorias, but spare a few minutes to take in the city views from Areopagus Hill before walking down towards Anafiótika.
4. Just off Theorías, visit the Kanellópoulos Museum and stop for lunch at one of the tavernas in Anafiótika.

Athens at a Glance

5. Explore the many churches and narrow streets of Anafiótika before making your way down Tripodon towards Plateía Lysikrátous.
6. Admire the Monument of Lysikrátous, perhaps over an afternoon drink in one of the nearby cafés.
7. Continue to Hadrian's Arch and the Temple of Olympian Zeus before turning right towards the Akropoli Metro.

Pláka and Monastiráki

Start/end: Syntagma Metro
1. Watch the parading guards outside Parliament House, then walk through Syntagma Square.
2. Turn left on Stadíou, right on Mitropóleos, then left on Nikis.
3. Enter the pedestrianized area on Kydathineon; visit the Greek Folk Art Museum, browse for souvenirs or have a coffee.
4. Turn right along Adrianoú, stopping at the Museum of Greek Popular Musical Instruments.
5. Continue straight towards the Ancient Agora where you will need at least a couple of hours to take in the sites and the museum.
6. Backtrack to the Roman Agora and enjoy a late lunch in one of the nearby restaurants.
7. Spend some time viewing the Tower of the Winds, then head north along Aiolou.
8. Turn right into Pandrósou, pausing to admire the Mitrópoli cathedral and the church of Panagía Gorgoepíkoös, before continuing on towards Syntagma Square.

3
Attica South

Attica, the region surrounding Athens, has plenty to tempt day-trippers from the city. Some of the highlights of the southern parts of Attica lie on the outskirts of the capital and can easily be reached by public transport. For others you will need to hire a car or join an organized tour.

Just east of Athens is **Moní Kaisarianí**, a beautiful little Byzantine monastery hidden among trees on the western slopes of **Mount Ymittós** – a world away from the hustle and bustle of the city.

Two main routes head south towards the tip of Attica. The most popular follows the coast, passing several **beach resorts**, before reaching **Cape Soúnion** with its dramatic **Temple of Poseidon**. Another route loops inland above Mount Ymittós, before turning south towards the pleasant towns of **Paiania** and **Markópoulo**. At the latter, a diversion east takes you to the ancient sanctuary of **Vravróna** where the mysterious bear dance was performed in honour of the goddess, Artemis.

Pórto Ráfti (a small resort) and **Lávrio** (an ancient silver-mining centre) are south of here. Otherwise, this is a quiet coastline, dotted with tavernas and rocky coves – a complete contrast to the hectic and crowded port of **Piraeus**. Immediately south of Athens, Piraeus has long since merged with the city's southern suburbs. A metro line provides a quick connection between the two – handy if you want to catch a ferry to one of the Saronic Gulf islands or stay and enjoy a meal at **Tourkolímano** – the more peaceful and picturesque of Piraeus' three harbours.

Don't Miss

*** **Moní Kaisarianí:** peaceful monastery surrounded by trees on the slopes of Mount Ymittós.
*** **Cape Soúnion:** site of the evocative Temple of Poseidon.
** **Vravróna:** remains of a sanctuary dedicated to the goddess of wild animals.
* **Vouliagméni:** one of several coastal resorts south of Athens.
* **Tourkolímano:** harbour in Piraeus lined with seafood tavernas.

Opposite: *A fisherman tends his nets at Pasalimá harbour in Piraeus.*

Above: *Tucked among trees on the slopes of Mt Ymittós, Kaisarianí Monastery is just a short drive east of Athens.*

Around Mount Ymittós

Providing a peaceful refuge from the city, Mount Ymittós (Hymettos) lies just east of Athens and reaches a high point of 1026m (3366ft). It is dotted with natural springs and caves and carpeted with fragrant herbs that have long been renowned for producing fine honey. However, the region is perhaps best known for the numerous monasteries that are found among its wooded foothills.

Moní Kaisarianí **

Out of sight and sound of hectic Athens, this serene monastery, set in lush grounds on the western slopes of Mount Ymittós, was founded in the 11th century. It derives its name from the so-called Imperial (*kaisariane*) Spring that Emperor Hadrian harnessed to provide water for the city during Roman times. The spring water, which still gushes from a Roman marble ram's head in the monastery's outer wall, was once thought to cure infertility.

In its heyday during the 12th and 13th centuries, Kaisarianí was home to 300 monks. Their cells, refectory and bathhouse can still be seen today. The most impressive building, however, is the ***katholikón*** dedicated to the Presentation of the Virgin. Built on the site of an ancient temple, it contains frescoes dating from the 16th and 17th centuries.

The monastery enjoyed special privileges during Ottoman occupation following the abbot's gift to Sultan Mehmed II of the keys to the city. It went into decline in the late 18th century and was not restored until 1956. The surrounding woodland of plane, cypress, and pine trees owes its existence to the Athens Tree Society which replanted the area after it was deforested during World

Pausanias (2nd century bc)

Background: Greek traveller and geographer.
Achievements: writing the *Guide to Greece* (in ten books) – a guide to the topography and antiquities of Greece.
Best known for: writing the first ever travel guide.

War II. Stroll a short distance above the monastery and you will find the ruins of an Early Christian church from where there are sweeping views over Athens.

Located 5km (3 miles) east of Athens, the monastery is open 08:30–15:00 Tuesday–Sunday; the grounds are open from sunrise to sunset.

Paiania ★

A quiet town on the eastern slopes of Mount Ymittós, Paiania's main attraction is the **Vorrés Museum** (open Saturday and Sunday) which houses an extensive private collection of art, from ancient sculpture to contemporary movements.

Paiania also boasts an interesting church, **Zoodóchos Pigí**, renowned for its fine frescoes.

Koutoúki Cave (open 09:00–16:00, daily) is 4km (2.5 miles) west of the town. Found in 1926 by a shepherd looking for a lost sheep, the cave's spectacular stalagmites and stalactites can be viewed on regular tours.

Piraeus

Lying 10km (6 miles) from central Athens, Piraeus is one of the biggest ports in the Mediterranean. Most tourists

Attica Wine Tour

The Attica Wine Growers Association, tel: 210 922 3105, organizes tours to vineyards participating in the Wine Roads of Attica programme. Visits to some of the region's archaeological sites are also included on itineraries. More information on greek wines can be found at www.greekwine.gr

Below: The Prayer of Joachim and Anne, *one of the many fine 16th- and 17th-century frescoes inside Kaisarianí Monastery.*

use Piraeus as a transit point for ferries to and from the Saronic islands (*see* page 109) and beyond. However, the city is not without its own attractions. There are interesting museums, some impressive neoclassical architecture and one or two picturesque harbours. Don't expect much in the way of a laid-back Greek seaside retreat, though. Piraeus is basically Athens-on-sea.

History

Piraeus was first settled around 500BC when Themistocles began building long defensive walls from Athens to the coast of the Saronic Gulf. More fortifications surrounded the port's three harbours which were lined with ship sheds and storerooms. The Spartans made short work of these during the Peloponnesian War in 404BC. New defences went up only to be torn down again in 88BC by the Roman commander, Sulla. Piraeus sank into obscurity, becoming little more than a fishing backwater by the Middle Ages – a far cry from the noisy, bustling city-port that merges with modern-day Athens.

Below: *Busy streets surround the main harbour at Piraeus.*

Exploring the City

Travelling to Piraeus by metro from Monastiráki in central Athens only takes about 20 minutes. The **market** area

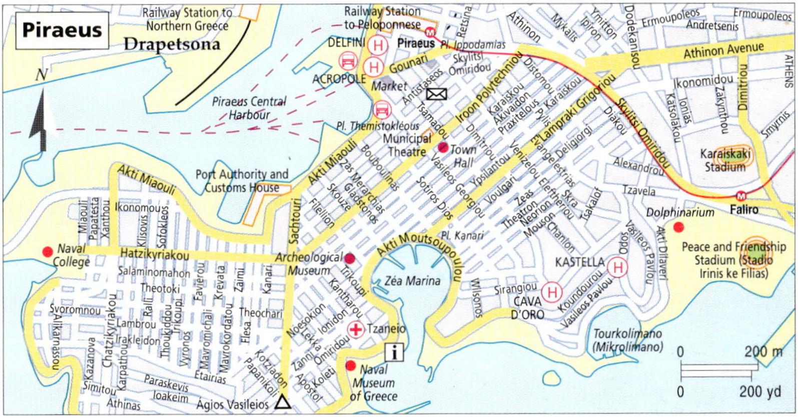

near the metro and railway stations has seafood, fruit and vegetable stalls, while on Sundays a flea market operates around the antique shops near Plateía Ippodamias.

It is a short walk from the station to the main ferry port, **Kentrikó Limáni**, where dozens of ferries, hydrofoils, catamarans and other passenger vessels crowd the wharf. Streets leading away from the harbour have some fine neoclassical buildings, including the **Town Hall** and **Municipal Theatre** – the latter houses the Municipal Art Gallery and the Museum of Stage Décor.

Walk uphill along Merarchias and through Plateía Terpsitheas and you will soon come to **Pasalimá** (or Zéa Marina), a horseshoe-shaped bay that used to be one of Themistocles' major naval ports with dry docks for hundreds of triremes. The Ottoman Fleet also moored here, but now the harbour is crammed with yachts and luxury launches, as well as a few fishing caïques.

Nearby, there are signs to the **Archaeological Museum** and the **Naval Museum of Greece** – both worth a visit. Another harbour, **Tourkolímano** (also known as Mikrolímano or Little Harbour), is found to the east – along with a dolphinarium and the Peace and Friendship Stadium. Quieter and more relaxing than the other harbours, Tourkolímano is lined with waterside tavernas serving tasty seafood dishes.

THE OLIVE TREE

- The olive tree, *Olea europaea*, can grow to 9m (30ft) in height and live to more than 1000 years old.
- Olive branches have come to symbolize fertility, honour, longevity, maturity, peace, prosperity purification, victory and wealth.
- In ancient Greece, the winners of the Olympic Games were given olive wreaths as trophies.
- According to Greek mythology, Athena gave the olive to mankind as a gift and as a result Athens was named in her honour.
- It was believed that the ancient Greek gods were born under olive branches.

Right: *Flying Dolphin ferries ply routes between Piraeus and the islands of the Saronic Gulf.*
Opposite: *The Naval Museum of Greece has displays depicting many of the country's great maritime battles.*

Sea Turtle Rescue Centre

Turtles, such as the leatherback and loggerhead, are at risk throughout the Mediterranean from pollution, boat collision and entanglement in fishing nets. The Sea Turtle Rescue Centre cares for injured turtles found in Greek waters. Located near Glyfáda's main square, it is open 10:00–14:00 and 17:00–19:00, daily.

Archaeological Museum *

Five magnificent bronze statues found near Piraeus' cathedral in 1959 are the star exhibits at this museum. They include the **Piraeus *kouros***, a 520BC statue of the god Apollo (the earliest full-length bronze statue to be discovered in Greece), as well as figures of Athena and Artemis. The museum also houses a cult statue of the earth goddess Cybele and some imposing funerary stelae. Created in 325BC, the **Monument of Nikeratos** is the largest grave monument ever found, measuring 7m (24ft) in height. Close to the museum are the remains of the **Theatre of Zéa** dating back to the 2nd century BC. The museum is located at 31 Chariláou Trikoúpi; open 08:30–14:30 Tuesday–Sunday.

Naval Museum of Greece *

Founded in 1949, this museum traces the maritime history of Greece from ancient to modern times. As well as flags, maps, uniforms and model boats, there are paintings of seascapes and plans of great naval campaigns. One of the most famous of these, the 480BC Battle of Sálamis, is depicted in a dramatic diorama. One of the rooms in the museum is built around an original section of **Themistocles' Long Walls**, while a more recent historical relic, the *Averof* (flagship of the Greek fleet until 1951) is moored nearby. Aktí Themistokléous near Freatyda Square, open 09:00–14:00 Tuesday–Saturday.

South to the Cape

The enticing, coast-hugging road winding south from Piraeus to Cape Soúnion makes a fascinating excursion that is full of eye-openers – both ancient and modern. Sometimes referred to as the Apollo Coast (after a small temple that was found near Vouliagméni), this route links a chain of popular beaches, lively resorts and quiet coves before culminating in the 'sacred cape' at the southern tip of Attica. It was here that the Athenians built sanctuaries to their two most important deities – Poseidon and Athena. The distance from Athens to Cape Soúnion is approximately 75km (47 miles) and a typical journey by tour coach takes around 1½ hours.

Homer (ca.8th century BC)

Background: Greek epic poet.
Achievements: being the traditional author of the *Iliad* and *Odyssey*.
Best known for: being the greatest poet of later antiquity.

Coastal Resorts ★

Crowded at weekends, particularly during summer, the resorts between Piraeus and Vouliagméni have plenty of amenities, ranging from marinas and water sports to hotels and sandy beaches. Nearest to Piraeus is **Paleo Fáliro**, home of the Fáliron Coastal Zone Olympic Complex, as well as a war cemetery dedicated to 2800 British soldiers who died in World War II. Further along the coast is the site of the old international airport in the suburb of **Glyfáda** – now a trendy suburb with a golf course, marina, boutiques, galleries and bars. The road then passes through **Voúla** which has

Poseidon (Greek myth)

Background: god of water and earthquakes.
Achievements: controlling the monsters of the sea and reputedly fathering the winged horse, Pegasus.
Best known for: his trident that could trigger huge waves, earthquakes, floods and volcanic eruptions.

two pay beaches. **Vouliagméni**, with its exclusive hotels, villas and a large yacht marina, is further down the coast and has another pay beach as well as a thermal lake. **Várkiza**, a wide sandy bay popular with windsurfers, is just around the corner. Roads lead inland from here to **Vári**, renowned for its meat tavernas. Beyond Várkiza, the route south becomes less developed with numerous coves and a spattering of villages and market towns, such as **Anavissos**.

Cape Soúnion ***

The winding coastal road from Piraeus is a great suspense-builder, hiding Cape Soúnion until you round a final bend and first glimpse the rocky headland with the **Temple of Poseidon** perched on top. There is no question as to why this site was chosen as a place to worship the mighty god of the sea. Particularly striking at sunset, the Doric temple, dating back to the 5th century BC, commands supreme views across the azure waters of the Aegean.

Below: *A wonderful sight as you round a bend on the coastal road from Piraeus, the Temple of Poseidon crowns Cape Soúnion.*

Only 15 of the original 34 columns remain. Erosion by wind, rain and sea-spray has inevitably taken its toll – although it is interesting to note that each column was cut with only 16 flutings (instead of the usual 20) to reduce the surface area exposed to the elements. Sadly, the columns have also been ravaged by 'human erosion' in the form of graffiti. Look closely and you may be able to spot the engraved initials of Lord Byron who visited in 1810.

Above: *Named after the god of the sea, the Temple of Poseidon is a popular excursion from Athens.*

The Temple of Poseidon was constructed on the site of a much earlier sanctuary. *Kouros* statues excavated here have been dated to the early 6th century BC and there is even evidence that the cape may have been some kind of cult centre as far back as Mycenaean times.

Today's visitors are justifiably drawn to the Temple of Poseidon, but there are many other intriguing aspects of the cape that are easily overlooked. The path leading from the tourist centre to the temple crosses the remains of **fortified walls** that were built in 412BC to protect the strategically positioned cape during the Peloponnesian War. On the west side of the headl and are the ruins of ancient **shipyards** that would have sheltered a pair of warships – no doubt to safeguard the passage of ships carrying grain to Athens. On a small hill slightly inland from the headland are the equally scant remains of the **Sanctuary of Athena Sounias**. Two temples are preserved here – the larger of which contained a cult statue of the goddess. Located 9km (5.5 miles) south of Lávrio, open from 10:00 until sunset daily.

HERODOTUS (*ca.*485–425BC)

Background: Greek historian and geographer.
Achievements: travelling the length of the ancient world, recording a wealth of facts and anecdotes.
Best known for: writing the *History*, an account of the wars between Greece and Persia.

The Southeast

An alternative route to the southern tip of Attica is to take the inland road across the Mesógeia plain towards the ancient silver-mining centre of **Lávrio**. En route you will pass **Paiania** (*see* page 83) and then **Markópoulo**, a pleasant market town with enticing cafés and a reputation for producing fine retsina. From Markópoulo a road heads east towards the coast and the small resort of **Pórto Ráfti**. Just offshore is the island of **Ráfti** with its Roman marble statue that was once used as a beacon to guide ships into the harbour. There are also several archaeological remains on the mainland near Pórto Ráfti, including Mycenaean tombs and a fortress from the 3rd century BC. **Vravróna**, with its ancient sanctuary, is also nearby, while further north lies the port of **Rafína** where you may be tempted to hop on a hydrofoil or ferry to nearby **Évia** (*see* fact panel on page 104) or, a little further away, the islands of **Andros**, **Tinos** or even **Mykonos**.

Lávrio *

Silver mined at Lávrio swelled the treasury of ancient Athens to such an extent that, without it, Pericles would have been unable to finance his ambitious building programme – and nor would Themistocles have been able to construct his fleet of 200 triremes (that proved their worth against the Persians at the Battle of Sálamis). The **Mineralogical Museum** (Andrea Kordela, open 10:00–12:00 Wednesday, Saturday and Sunday) delves into the history and geology of the area, displaying many kinds of minerals – including some retrieved from ancient slag heaps that have since become submerged by the sea. Nearby, the **Archaeological Museum** (open 10:00–15:00 Wednesday–Monday) displays the remains of the frieze from the Temple of Poseidon.

Vravróna **

In the 5th century BC, Vravróna (or Ancient Brauron) was a sanctuary dedicated to Artemis, goddess of wild animals. The foundations of the Doric-style **Temple of Artemis** can be seen, as well as the **Sacred House** where

Rafína

The second biggest port in Attica (after Piraeus), Rafína has regular ferry and high-speed catamaran services to the Cyclades. Catamarans take two hours to Mykonos and three to Paros.

the cult's priestesses lived. The most intact monument is the colonnaded **stoa** (sometimes rather grandly called the Parthenon of the Bear Maidens) where young girls from well-to-do families came to honour the goddess. Dressed in saffron robes, they performed the mysterious 'bear dance' in the hope that Artemis would look kindly on them. Also worth seeing at the site are the remains of an ancient **stone bridge**. There is an excellent **museum** nearby displaying statues of the bear maidens, numerous dedications to Artemis and other local finds. Located some 10km (6 miles) northeast of Markópoulo, open 08:30–14:45 Tuesday–Sunday.

RETSINA

Since ancient times, the resin of the Aleppo pine has been added to grape juice during the fermentation process in order to preserve and flavour retsina. Despite advances made by Attica's 'traditional' wine growers, retsina remains a popular drink in Greece. The Mesógeia region of Attica is renowned for its retsina with major producers, such as Kourtákis, owning vineyards in Markópoulo and Koropí.

Left: *The Parthenon of the Bear Maidens forms the most extensive remains at the 5th century* BC *site of Vravróna.*

Attica South at a Glance

Best Times to Visit

Many Athenians find refuge from the city's summer heat by spending weekends and holidays in the coastal resorts of Glyfáda, Vouliagméni and Voúla. Accommodation may be difficult to find during the busiest periods and beaches may be crowded. Try to visit Moní Kaisarianí in the week since it is busy on weekends. Cape Soúnion is impressive at sunset when the Temple of Poseidon is silhouetted against a rose-tinted Aegean Sea.

Getting There

To Moní Kaisarianí: Take bus 224 from Plateía Kaningos, Akadimías, and walk 2km (1.2 miles) uphill to the monastery.
To Piraeus and coastal resorts: From the international airport take the E96 airport bus to Piraeus via Glyfáda – a 24hr service every 15–30min. The bus stops at Plateía Karaiskáki near the harbour in Piraeus. From central Athens take Metro Line 1. The journey from Monastiráki station takes around 20min. The metro station in Piraeus is a five-minute walk from the harbour. Bus 040 departs from Filellínon Street in Athens and stops at Plateía Karaiskáki near the harbour in Piraeus, while bus 049 leaves Omónia Square bound for Plateía Themistokléos in Piraeus. The A2 express bus from Plateía Syntagma goes to Glyfáda, Voúla and Vouliagméni. A tramway along Syngroú to Glyfáda is under construction. Piraeus is connected by train to the Peloponnese (the station is near the metro terminal) and parts of northern Greece. Piraeus is a major hub for ferry travel. In summer, international ferries operate between Piraeus and Cyprus (Lemesos), Rhodes and Israel (Haifa). Local ferries, catamarans and hydrofoils ply routes to and from the islands of the Saronic Gulf, *see* page 109.
To Cape Soúnion: The coastal bus from Mavromatéon Terminal in Athens leaves hourly until 17:30 and takes 2hr to reach the Cape. The inland bus takes slightly longer and travels via Paiania, Markópoulo and Lávrio. Several companies offer tours to the Cape.
To Rafína: There is a bus from the airport to the port of Rafína every 40min from 06:00–21:30. Frequent buses also depart from Mavromatéon Terminal in Athens. Ferries and catamarans operate between Rafína and Andros, Tinos and Mykonos, Lésvos (Limnos) and Évia (Marmari and Karystos).
To other locations: Buses for **Pórto Ráfti** depart every 30–60min from Mavromatéon Terminal in Athens. The A5 bus leaves for **Paiania** from Akadimías. To reach **Vravróna**, take Metro Line 2 to Ethnikí Ámina, then 306 bus to Artemis-Loútsa – a 1km (0.6-mile) walk from the archaeological site.

Getting Around

In Piraeus, bus 904 links the metro station with Pasalimá (Zéa Marina). Buses A1 and B1 leave for Glyfáda from near the port of Piraeus. Buses 114, 115 and 116 depart from Glyfáda for Voúla and Vouliagméni.

Where to Stay

Piraeus

Luxury

Kastella, 75 Vasileos Pávlou, tel: 210 411 4735. Good views of Tourkolímano.
Cava d'Oro, 19 Vasileos Pávlou, tel: 210 412 2210. Comfortable rooms and a popular bar and disco; overlooks Tourkolímano harbour.

Mid-range

Lilia, 131 Zéas, Passalimáni, tel: 210 417 9108. Clean and comfortable hotel; provides free transport to the port.

Budget

Achillion, 63 Notára, tel: 210 412 4029. *En-suite* rooms are available at this simple hotel.

Glyfáda

Luxury

Oasis, 27 Poseidónos, tel: 210 894 1742. Some of the two-room apartments overlook the beach. Pools and a jacuzzi.

Mid-range

Zina, 6 Evangelistras, tel: 210 960 3872. Well-equipped apartments in a quiet location.

Vouliagméni

Luxury

Aphrodite Astir Palace, 40 Apollonos, tel: 210 890 2000.

Attica South at a Glance

Resort hotel on the peninsula with beaches, bars, water sports and a health club.

Cape Soúnion

Mid-range

Saron, 4km (2.5 miles) from the Cape, tel: 229 203 9144. Lovely setting among pine trees, this hotel has comfortable rooms and a pool.

Where to Eat

Piraeus

Luxury

Istioploikos, Tourkolímano (Mikrolímano), tel: 210 413 4084. Fresh seafood on a moored ship in the harbour.

Jimmy the Fish, 46 Akti Koumoundourou, tel: 210 412 4417. Taverna along the waterfront at Tourkolímano; excellent seafood – the lobster spaghetti is a house speciality.

Varoúlko, 14 Deligorgi, tel: 210 411 2043. An excellent seafood taverna using local ingredients in wonderfully creative dishes.

Mid-range

Archaion Gefsis, 10 Epidavrou, tel: 210 413 8617. Eat like an ancient Greek in this atmospheric and fun themed restaurant.

Margaró, 126 Hatzikyriákou, tel: 210 451 4226. Seafood taverna, popular with locals and tourists alike.

Alli Skála, 57 Serifou, tel: 210 482 7722. Traditional dishes served in a courtyard filled with banana trees.

Glyfáda

Mid-range

Far East, Lazaraki and Pandoras, tel: 210 894 0500. Excellent Chinese restaurant with a reputation for delicious Peking duck.

Budget

O Tzórtzis, 4 Konstantinoupóleos, tel: 210 894 6020. Taverna serving tasty traditional food.

Vári

Mid-range

Ta Vlachika, 35 Leofóros Váris, tel: 210 895 6141. Specialize in meat grills, renowned for their spit-roasted lamb and suckling pig.

Vouliagméni

Luxury

Lámpros, 20 Leofóros Poseidónos, tel: 210 896 0144. Waterside restaurant offering fine seafood and an excellent wine list.

Bars and clubs

In summer, the cool crowd head to the coast where clubs like **Budha**, in Glyfáda, and **Island**, in Várkiza, provide music and drinks by the sea.

Shopping

The flea market in Piraeus is centred on Alipedou, behind the metro station, and is open 07:00–14:00 Sun. As well as the usual junk and bric-a-brac stalls, there are shops selling antiques, jewellery and other collectable items.

Beaches

The pay beaches in the resorts south of Athens have good facilities, including changing rooms, snack bars and toilets. **Alimo**, 08:00–21:00, waterslide, canoeing and tennis; **Voúla**, 07:00–20:00, waterslide; **Vouliagméni**, 08:00–21:00, water sports and cafés; **Várkiza**, 08:00–20:00, exclusive development, facilties include jet skis and tennis. **Limni Vouliagméni**, 06:30–20:00 summer and 07:30–17:00 winter, is a thermal lake believed to have therapeutic properties. A popular year-round swimming location.

Useful Contacts

Tourist Information: Hellenic Tourism Organisation (EOT), Pasalimá (Zéa Marina), Piraeus, tel: 210 452 2586, open 08:00–15:00 Mon–Fri.

Currency exchange, **National Bank of Greece**, cnr Antistaseos and Tsamadou, near Kentrikó Limáni (main ferry port), Piraeus.

Post Office, cnr Tsamadou and Filonos, Piraeus, open 07:30–20:00 Mon–Fri, 07:30–14:00 Sat.

Port police, Piraeus, tel: 210 412 2501.

Aegean Dive Centre, 53 Zamanou, Glyfáda, tel: 210 894 5409. Dive sites are mainly along the Apollo coast.

Glyfáda Golf Course, Glyfáda, tel: 210 894 6820; 18-hole public course.

4
North from Athens

Major highways (the E75 and E94) head north and west from Athens towards Thessaloníki and Corinth, respectively. The western route gropes through an unsightly sprawl of factories and oil refineries, but persevere and you will find two historical gems – **Dáfní Monastery**, with its stunning Byzantine mosaics, and **Ancient Eleusis**, the ruins of a major centre of cult worship dating from around 2000BC. The legendary pilgrimage route of the Sacred Way once led from here to the Kerameikós of Athens.

Just 20km (12 miles) to the north of the city lies **Mount Párnitha National Park** – a popular weekend escape for Athenians that offers some good walking trails and plenty of opportunities for bird-watching. To the northeast of Athens is the bay of **Marathon** where, against all the odds, the Greeks defeated the Persians in 490BC. A short distance north of the village of Marathonás (the starting point of the original marathon race) are the peaceful ruins of **Rámnous**. This ancient sanctuary (and another called the **Amphiáraion** further along the coast) has beautiful views towards the island of Évia.

Most people heading north out of Athens on a day trip are bound for **Delphi** – regarded by ancient Greeks as the centre of the world. Although well beyond the borders of Attica, the breathtaking combination of mountain scenery and well-preserved ruins at this spiritual centre more than compensate for the long drive.

Don't Miss

*** **Dáfní Monastery:** famed for its stunning Byzantine mosaics.
*** **Delphi:** a long day trip north of Attica, but worth it for remarkable ruins in a beautiful mountain setting.
** **Ancient Eleusis:** intriguing ruins of an ancient cult centre.
* **Marathon:** a famous battle site.
* **Mount Párnitha:** popular retreat from the city.

Opposite: *At the cemetery of Dáfní Monastery there is a 9th-century chapel dedicated to Saint Nicolas.*

THE SACRED WAY

It always helps to approach an ancient ruin with a good dose of imagination – and **Ancient Eleusis** is no exception. However, as you leave Athens on the busy Corinth highway that passes the remains of this extraordinary religious centre (crowded by the industrial mayhem of modern-day Elefsína), it's hard to ignore the factories, oil refineries and dockyards of the city's western suburbs. It all seems a far cry from the Sacred Way that once linked Athens with Eleusis. Nevertheless, this is still a worthwhile excursion, particularly when combined with the beautiful Byzantine monastery of **Dáfní**.

EARTHQUAKE

On 7 September 1999, an earthquake measuring 5.9 on the Richter Scale struck Athens, killing 139 inhabitants and leaving over 100,000 homeless. It was the most powerful quake to affect the city in two centuries. Pottery toppled and smashed in the National Archaeology Museum, mosaics were damaged at Dáfní Monastery, and fragments of marble were dislodged from the Parthenon. Lying near the convergence of three tectonic plates (the Eurasian, African and Arabian), Greece has experienced more than 20,000 earthquakes in the last 40 years.

Dáfní Monastery ***

Founded in the 5th century AD, this well-known monastery is built on the site of an ancient sanctuary to Apollo that marked the point where the Sacred Way began its final approach to Eleusis. It takes its name from the laurels (*dáfnes*) that used to grow here. The ***katholikón*** (main church) was built ca.1080 and boasts a dome measuring 8m (26ft) in diameter and 16m (52ft) high. The **cloisters** were added in the 16th century following the arrival of Greek Orthodox monks.

Inside the *katholikón* are the exquisite and famous gold-leaf Byzantine **mosaics** – each one a masterpiece. The dome is dominated by a stern portrait of *Christ Pantokrátor* surrounded by the 16 prophets, while the ceiling is adorned with scenes of the *Nativity, Baptism, Transfiguration* and *Annunciation*. The walls of the *katholikón* depict saints, angels and other holy scenes, including the *Betrayal by Judas*, the *Washing of the Feet*, the *Last Supper*, and the *Resurrection*.

In 1999, an earthquake rocked the area, causing the *katholikón* to be closed for restoration work. It was the latest in a long series of blows to have afflicted the monastery, ranging from sacking by crusaders to desecration by Turks.

Located 10km (6 miles) northwest of Athens, the monastery is open 08:30–15:00 daily.

Ancient Eleusis **

Severed from the Acropolis by modern-day urban sprawl, Eleusis was once an intrinsic part of cult worship in ancient Athens. Founded ca.2000BC on the slopes of a hill, its strategic position led to the development of a large fortified settlement. Magnificent buildings embellished the site during Roman and classical periods, but the sanctuary was abandoned in the 4th century AD following the Gothic invasion and spread of Christianity.

Opposite: *The monks' cells were located across the courtyard of the cloisters at Dáfní Monastery.*
Below: The Betrayal by Judas, *one of the stunning Byzantine mosaics in Dáfní Monastery.*

Did You Know?

The custom of competing naked at the ancient Olympic Games probably arose from a scandal involving an athlete's mother infiltrating the men-only games disguised as his coach.

In its heyday, Eleusis attracted some 30,000 devotees. The focus of their worship was the myth of the grieving goddess, Demeter, whose daughter, Persephone, was abducted by Hades, god of the Underworld. Secret rituals and sacrifices took place as part of the so-called **Eleusinian Mysteries** (established during the 6th century BC). The Mysteries were the culmination of a nine-day annual festival that took place each September. It would begin with initiates (or *mystes*) presenting baskets of sacred offerings to the Eleusinion in Athens. The archon of Athens would then declare the festival open to any man or woman who was not a murderer, barbarian or non-Greek speaker. Initiates purified themselves in the sea and sacrificed piglets before setting off along the Sacred Way from Kerameikós (*see* page 43) to Eleusis in a procession followed by Athenian citizens and the 500 Areopagus civic council members. It was a lively parade, punctuated by plenty of stops for dancing, singing and, of course, more sacrifices. On arrival at Eleusis, initiates would be ushered

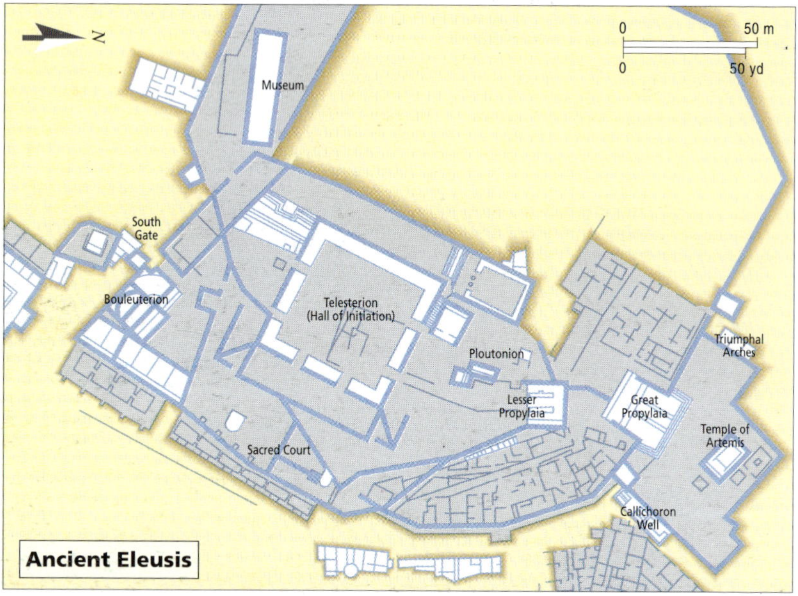

Ancient Eleusis

into the **Telesterion**, the Hall of Initiation, where the high priestess would perform her rites. Little is known about this most sacred of ceremonies – hardly surprising considering execution was the penalty for spilling the beans. It seems, however, that the priestess became a medium between initiates and gods and, in doing so, was able to reveal a (hopefully positive) vision of life after death.

Just as patchy and confusing are the monuments of Ancient Eleusis, so you may find it useful to begin your visit at the site's **museum** which contains reconstruction models, as well as some wonderful statues, amphorae and relief carvings dating from around 600BC.

Outside, foundations and eroded column bases trace the outlines of the Telesterion (an impressive building that had 42 columns and enough seating for 3000 initiates). Other finds at Eleusis include the **Greater Propylaia** (a temple from the 2nd century AD modelled on the one at the Acropolis), the **Sacred Court** (a gathering place for the pilgrims that marked the end of the Sacred Way), the **Callichoron Well** (where Demeter is said to have mourned for Persephone), the **Ploutonion** (a sanctuary to Hades located in a small cave), and a pair of **triumphal arches**.

Ancient Eleusis is located at Elefsína, 22km (14 miles) northwest of Athens; open 08:30–15:00 Tuesday–Sunday. Heading north from Elefsína will take you to the wine-making town of Inoí, beyond which lie the 4th century BC **Eleutherai Fortress** and the 11th-century Monastery of **Ósios Melétios**. To the east on the Halcyonic Gulf near Pórto Gérmeno is another fortress – the classical **Aigosthena**.

Sanctuaries of the North

Northern Attica contains several little-visited highlights that certainly warrant a day trip or two. All of them, in a way, are sanctuaries. **Mount Párnitha National Park** is a haven for wildlife; **Marathon** preserves a memorial to the casualties of the great Battle of Marathon, while **Rámnous** and the **Amphiáraion** (or **Oropós**) are both sites of ancient sanctuaries dedicated to gods or heroes.

Byzantine Art

Mosaics and frescoes in a Byzantine church have a symbolic arrangement from heaven to earth. The image of Christ Pantokrátor is always high in the dome. The Virgin is depicted in the semi-dome of the apse, while saints occupy the lower levels of the side walls.

Above: *Worry beads are available from souvenir shops throughout Athens.*

Mount Párnitha National Park ★

Traffic permitting, it takes less than an hour to drive from Athens to this rugged national park. Mount Párnitha (or Parnés) is Attica's highest peak at 1413m (4636ft). Its lower slopes are swathed in typical maquis vegetation which graduates higher up into Aleppo pine and then Greek fir. Wild **flowers** are abundant (especially spring crocus and autumn cyclamen), while **birds** include several species of raptor ranging from peregrine falcons to golden eagles (if you're lucky). Plenty of **walking** trails crisscross the park – the most popular being the two-hour jaunt from Thrakomakedónes to the Bafí refuge.

The main centre from which to explore Mount Párnitha is **Ágia Triáda**, a small resort at 1100m (3600ft). The mountain road continues from here to the summit and there's also a less frequented path leading to the Cave of Pan.

To the west of Mount Párnitha National Park are the ruins of the **Fortress of Phyle**, constructed in the 4th century BC to guard an ancient road between Athens and Thebes. To reach it, you will pass the settlement of **Filí** (which makes a good lunch stop) and **Goúra Gorge** – the precipitous home of 17th-century **Moní Klistón**.

Marathon ★

The **Marathon Tomb** (signposted after the Golden Coast Hotel, open 08:30–15:00 Tuesday–Sunday) contains the cremated remains of the Athenians who died fending off a Persian invasion during the Battle of Marathon in 490BC. The burial mound, which measures 10m (35ft) in height, once held a victorious statue of Nike – and what a victory it was.

When 25,000 Persians arrived in the bay **of Marathon**, Athens must have thought the game was up. Despite forcing freed slaves into battle garb and dispatching a runner, Pheidippides, to Sparta to seek reinforcements, the city could only muster an army of 10,000 (Plataea sent 1000 men, while Sparta's forces arrived a day late).

Outnumbered by more than two to one, the Greeks took up a strategic hilltop position and a four-day stand-off ensued. When the Persians finally made their move one of the generals of the Greek army, Militiades, launched a swift counter-manoeuvre that caught the invaders by surprise. Perhaps its was Militiades' inside knowledge (he had formerly served as a mercenary in Persia's army), but the Greeks suddenly had the upper hand. An hour later, 6400 Persians lay slain – in stark contrast to the 192 Athenians who perished.

The story goes (and it may well be just popular myth) that poor old Pheidippides was dispatched once again – this time to relay news of the victory back to Athens. Upon arrival in the Ancient Agora, he gasped '*Nenikíamen*!' (victory is ours) and promptly died of exhaustion. His heroic efforts, however, have since been immortalized in the marathon – an international sporting event that faithfully covers the 42km (26 miles) that Pheidippides supposedly ran between the battlefield and Athens. The rural village of **Marathónas** has a platform marking the annual marathon race to the capital.

Marathon Museum displays artefacts from the area, ranging from ceramic offerings discovered at the Marathon Tomb to fine Egyptian-style statues from the estate of Roman benefactor Herodes Atticus who hailed from nearby. **Marathon Lake** lies 8km (5 miles) west of Marathónas and was formed in 1931 by a dam – unique in the world for its outer facing of Pentelic marble.

Rámnous *

Tucked away in a remote and picturesque corner of northeast Attica, Rámnous (open 08:00–18:00, daily) was the only Greek sanctuary dedicated to Nemesis, the goddess of vengeance. Little remains of the two

Church Terminology

Iconostasis: screen, embellished with icons, that separates the altar from the rest of the church.
***Katholikón*:** main church of a monastery complex.
Narthex: porch of a church.
Sacristy: room where sacred vessels are kept.

Post-haste

Spíros Loúis, a postman from Maroússi, won the first marathon of the modern Olympics in 1896 when he ran the 24.8 miles from Marathon to the Kallimármaro Stadium in Athens in two hours, 58 minutes and 50 seconds.

temples at the site. The larger **Temple of Nemesis** was built in the mid-5th century BC and once contained a cult statue of the goddess done in Parian marble. Archaeologists have reconstructed part of its base which, together with fragments of the temple's pediment, can be seen in the nearby **museum**. An **ancient road** leading to Rámnous has also been excavated. Just north of the sanctuary is a **fortress** constructed during the Peloponnesian War to protect ships passing through the narrow and vulnerable straits between Attica and the island of Évia. Today, ferries cross the straits, leaving from the small port of **Ágia Marína**.

The Amphiáraion *

Like Rámnous, the Amphiáraion (or Ancient Oropós) occupies a secluded, peaceful spot where you may find yourself contemplating the solitude and wildlife as much as the archaeological remains. In antiquity, people were drawn here to receive the healing powers of Amphiaraos who was said to have been born from the site's **sacred spring**. The base of a cult statue can still be discerned among the ruins of a Doric **temple**, built in the 4th century BC. There are also the remains of an **altar** where the sick would sacrifice a ram before seeking Amphiaraos' aid. The rather grisly rite would then involve the devotees wrapping themselves in the ram's skin and sleeping in the long stoa-like **Enkoimeterion** while priests analysed their dreams. Other ruins at the Amphiáraion include a **theatre** and **water clock**. Located north of Kálamos, it is open from 08:00–14:30 Tuesday–Sunday.

Nearby are the coastal villages of Ág. Apóstoli and Skála Oropoú, the latter of which has regular ferries to Erétria on the island of Évia.

The Road to Delphi

Well beyond the borders of Attica, lying 178km (110 miles) and a three-hour drive northwest of Athens, **Delphi** is one of the most popular excursions from the capital. Whether you join an organized tour or rent a car,

Delphi Stadium

The stadium at Delphi is one of the best preserved in Greece. It was used as the venue for the Pythian Games which were held every four years. Originally a musical festival, the games had an athletic component from 582BC. Victors were awarded a laurel wreath and the right to have their statue erected in the Sanctuary of Apollo.

you cannot fail to be moved by Delphi's fascinating ancient ruins and sublime mountain setting. The E75 National Highway curves north and then west from Athens.

After about 85km (53 miles), a turn-off leads to the legendary city of **Thebes** which is now renowned for its **Archaeology Museum** (open from 09:00–15:00 Tuesday–Sunday). From Thebes, a road continues in a westerly direction to **Livadiá** where you can stop next to the source of the Erkyna River – a beautiful spot with waterfalls, pools, cafés and a small museum. After Livadiá the road begins to climb into the mountains.

A diversion to the left takes you to the 11th-century **Monastery of Ósios Loukás** (open 08:00–14:00 and 16:00–19:00 May–September; 08:00–17:00 October–April) perched on Mount Helicon. Views aside, the outstanding gold mosaics inside Ósios Loukás more than warrant the side trip. Back on the road to Delphi, you next reach the ski resort of **Aráchova** – a mountain town that's also famous for rugs and goat's cheese. After a few kilometres skirting the flank of **Mount Parnassós** you finally reach Delphi.

Above: *The belltower of the Monastery of Ósios Loukás with the slopes of Mount Elikonas in the background.*

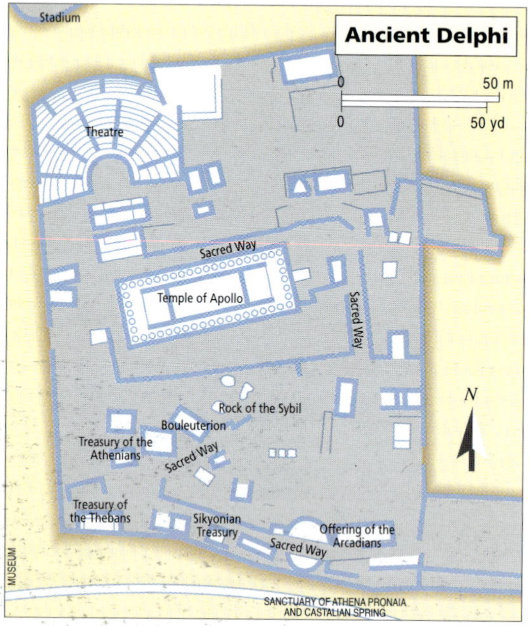

Ancient Delphi

According to myth, Apollo reached Delphi by turning himself into a dolphin (hence the name Delphi). Another legend – of Zeus releasing two eagles from opposite ends of the world and their paths crossing over Delphi – firmly established the sanctuary at the very epicentre of spirituality in the ancient world. Pilgrims from as far as Egypt and Persia visited the oracles at Delphi to consult with the gods. From common man to powerful ruler, no mortal would consider making an important decision before hearing what Apollo had to say about it.

History

Delphi's history dates back to Mycenaean times when Gaia, the Earth goddess, was worshipped here. The late 8th century BC witnessed the development of the **Sanctuary of Apollo** and the rise to fame of the **Delphic Oracle**. During the 6th century BC, Delphi began hosting the **Pythian Games** which included music, athletics and chariot racing. The sanctuary entered a golden age, its reputation blossoming and its buildings growing ever more grander. When the Romans arrived, however, the sparkle began fading. Sulla pillaged the treasury in 83BC and even when Hadrian and Herodes Atticus splashed out on a renovation in the 2nd century AD it was mainly for the benefit of sightseeing Romans. The oracle last spoke sometime around AD360 before the cult was finally abolished in AD393 by Emperor Theodosius.

The Delphic Oracle

Induced by vapours seeping from a crack in the ground, the Delphic Oracle, or *Pythia* (a priestess over the age of 50), was revered for her ability to hear the words of the god Apollo. People came to Delphi from far and wide to ask the oracle for advice. Divinations were given on receipt of a levy (*pelanos*) and following the sacrifice of an animal.

Exploring the Site

Arriving from the direction of Aráchova, the first of Delphi's two main sacred areas that you will encounter is the **Sanctuary of Athena Pronaia** (or Marmaria Precinct). Further along the road is the **Castalian Spring** where the oracle, pilgrims and priests would cleanse themselves prior to any ceremony. The **Sanctuary of Apollo** (or Sacred Precinct) is nearby and contains the remains of numerous monuments linked by the winding **Sacred Way**. On a levelled area above the sanctuary is a well-preserved **stadium** with seating for 7000 and a track measuring 177m (580ft) in length. To the west of the sanctuary is the **museum** (open from 07:30–19:00 Monday–Friday, 08:30–15:00 Saturday and Sunday). The star exhibit is undoubtedly the bronze ***Charioteer*** which was commissioned in 478BC to commemorate a victory in the chariot races. Other must-sees include a detailed scale model of Delphi and a wealth of statues, friezes and other offerings from the treasuries in the Sanctuary of Apollo.

Below: *A long day trip north of Attica, the Sanctuary of Athena Pronaia is a must-see.*

Sanctuary of Athena Pronaia ***

The remains of two **temples** dedicated to the goddess, Athena Pronaia, can be found here (the oldest dates from the mid-7th century BC), but your eye will inevitably be drawn instead to the photogenic **Tholos**. This

ÉVIA

The second largest island in Greece, Évia can be reached by a short ferry crossing from the Attica ports of Rafína, Ágia Marina and Skala Oropou – or by bridge over the Evripous Channel to the island's capital, Halkida. Highlights for visitors to the island include scenic mountain roads, traditional villages and a beautiful coastline.

elegant rotunda was built ca.390BC. Three of its original 20 Doric columns have been re-erected, but the purpose of the building remains a mystery.

Sanctuary of Apollo ***

This extraordinary Sacred Precinct is riddled with ruins. From the moment you've bought your entrance ticket you are in the midst of a **Roman Agora** dating back to the 4th century AD. From here, the paved **Sacred Way** climbs past the first of numerous plinths that would have supported **monuments** to battle victories, such as Marathon (*see* page 101). Following these are the remains of 27 **treasuries** where offerings and war spoils were held. Next to the reconstructed **Treasury of the Athenians** is the **Rock of the Sybil** where, according to legend, Delphi's first oracle prophesied. At the top of the Sacred Way (after passing more pedestals for victory, bronzes and tripods), you reach the 4th century BC Doric **Temple of Apollo** – the most imposing structure at Delphi with six columns standing. Behind the temple is the 35-tier **theatre** from which the most beautiful views of Delphi and the surrounding mountain scenery can be enjoyed.

Below: *Although a temple has stood on this site since the 6th century BC, today's remains of the Temple of Apollo date from the 4th century BC.*

North from Attica at a Glance

Best Times To Visit

If you are a keen bird-watcher, a visit to Mount Párnitha during the spring and autumn migration seasons might be especially rewarding. Delphi is wonderful year-round, but can get overrun by tour coach parties in the busy summer months. Try timing your visit so that you can soak up the views and atmosphere of the ruins and mountain scenery during early morning or late in the afternoon.

Getting There

To Dáfní Monastery and Ancient Eleusis:
Take bus A16 from Plateía Eleftherias in Athens to Venzini which is located near the monastery. The journey only takes about about 30min, traffic permitting. The same bus continues on to Elefsína for Ancient Eleusis.

To Mount Párnitha National Park:
Bus 713 leaves from Acharnón, Omónia, at 06:30 and 14:30 to Ág. Triáda, while bus 914 departs from Plateía Váthis to the base of the funicular railway. Ág. Triáda is also accessible by road.

To Marathon, Rámnous and the Amphiáraion
Renting a car and driving yourself is the best option for reaching these archaeological sites. Although no buses will take you directly to them, there are services from Mavromatéon Terminal in Athens to Marathonás, Soúli (near Rámnous) and Kálamos (near the Amphiáraion).

To Delphi:
There are six daily buses from Athens' Liossion Terminal. The journey takes 3hr and buses can be very full in summer. Several companies in Athens offer full-day guided tours to Delphi, *see* page 77 for details.

Where to Stay

Mount Párnitha National Park

Luxury

Grand Hotel Mont Parnés, near Ág. Triáda, tel: 210 246 9111. Located at 1050m (3444ft), this hotel enjoys sweeping views across Attica and is also renowned for its casino, open 07:30–01:45 Thu–Tue.

Delphi

Luxury

Xenía, 69 Apóllonos, tel: 226 508 2151. Located just 600m (1968ft) from Ancient Delphi, this hotel has large rooms with balconies and an indoor swimming pool.

Pan, 53 Vas. Pávlou and Frederíkis, tel: 226 508 2320. Comfortable hotel offering family rooms, some with views.

Mid-range

Varónos, 25 Vas. Pávlou, tel: 226 508 2345. Clean and comfortable rooms with balconies. The spacious lobby has a profusion of plants.

Budget

Pension Sibylla, 9 Vas. Pávlou, tel: 226 508 2335. Simple, but pleasant and well-priced accommodation with *en-suite* rooms.

Apollon Camping, 1.5km (1 mile) west of Delphi, tel: 226 508 2750. A shop, barbecue area, swimming pool and restaurant makes this an excellent choice for travellers with their own camping gear.

Where to Eat

Mount Párnitha National Park

Mid-range

O Vlachos, Leoforos Parnithos, tel: 210 246 3762. Located in the foothills, this Greek taverna has a good selection of meat grills.

Delphi

Mid-range

Taverna Váchos, 31 Apóllonos, tel: 226 508 3186. An excellent taverna serving all the old favourites.

Useful Contacts

Tourist Information, Vas. Pávlou, Delphi, tel: 226 508 2900, open 07:30–14:30 Mon–Fri. Free map available.

PINE ISLAND
TOURIST OFFICE
TRAVEL AGENCY
FLYING DOLPHINS
bardakos tours
FLYING DOLPHINS
FACES

5
The Saronic Gulf Islands

Five main islands are scattered across the Saronic Gulf between Athens and the Peloponnese. All are popular holiday haunts for locals and tourists alike – but their laid-back atmosphere conceals a gritty past. **Sálamis**, nearest of the islands to Athens (and little more than a suburban extension) was the site of a crucial sea battle in 480BC between Athens and Persia. **Aegina** was once an ancient power base with a formidable navy that must have unnerved the rulers of Athens. Also boasting a strong maritime heritage, **Hydra** and **Spétses** spearheaded the Greek fleets in the War of Independence.

Along with **Póros**, all five islands are easily reached by ferry or hydrofoil from Piraeus. If time is limited, you can join a cruise boat that takes in two or three of the islands with a few hours spent on each.

There's plenty to see and do. The sight of picture-perfect **Hydra harbour** is guaranteed to revitalize the soul of the most city-bludgeoned traveller, while Póros is just a short hop from the enticing Peloponnese mainland. Aegina is perhaps the most interesting for sightseeing, with its beautifully preserved **Temple of Aphaia** and the intriguing ghost town of **Paleochóra**. Most people, however, head for the Saronic Gulf islands with very little in the way of an archaeological tick list. If, like them, you're looking for a sandy beach on which to unwind or a waterside taverna serving delicious fresh seafood, then this little cluster of Greek islands will fit the bill perfectly.

Don't Miss

*** **Hydra Town:** one of the most picturesque harbours in Greece.
** **Temple of Aphaia:** well-preserved temple on Aegina.
** **Beaches:** Póros and Spétses have some of the best beaches.
* **Paleochóra:** fascinating ghost town on Aegina.

Opposite: *Tiered rows of houses crowd the harbour at Hydra – a popular day-trip by ferry from Piraeus.*

WHALES AND DOLPHINS

The sea off southern Greece is home to several species of cetacean, including bottlenose, common and striped dolphins – all of which may be sighted during a cruise in the Saronic Gulf. Further offshore, the sea depth reaches 5.5km (3.5 miles) – deep enough for sperm whales and Cuvier's beaked whales which feed on deep-sea squid.

AEGINA

The humble pistachio nut (along with fishing and tourism) provides Aegina's modern-day bread and butter, but back in the 7th century BC the island was reaping the rewards of a healthy trade in pottery and perfume. Such was its success that, in 650BC, Aegina minted some of Europe's first coins. It also developed a formidable navy which played a hand in the Greek victory over the Persians at the Battle of Sálamis. Athens, however, eventually could no longer abide such a strong neighbour and took control in 458BC.

Today, Aegina is a popular seaside bolt hole for Athenians and can get very busy at weekends. **Aegina Town**, the island's main port, has a busy harbour lined with cafés and tavernas. The town was the capital of Greece for a few years after the War of Independence and some fine **neoclassical buildings** date from this period.

North of town is a small beach, beyond which lie the remains of the **Temple of Apollo**. A nearby **Archaeology Museum** (08:30–15:00 Tue–Sun) exhibits local artefacts. South of town is a **water park** (10:00–20:00 daily), while to the southwest is the **Hellenic Wildlife Rehabilitation Centre** (11:00–13:00 daily). **Perdika** fishing village, 21km (13 miles) south of town, has a small beach and popular fish tavernas. The island's main resort is Ágia Marina.

Below: *Tiers of houses sweep down to the harbour at Hydra – the perfect place for a drink or meal at one of the waterside restaurants.*

Temple of Aphaia **

Built ca.480BC, this magnificent temple (with 25 of its 32 columns still standing) was dedicated to the island's goddess. As well as being one of the best preserved Doric temples in Greece, its pine-covered hilltop position provides far-reaching views across the Saronic Gulf. Located 10km (6 miles) east of Aegina Town, the temple is open 08:30–17:00 Monday–Friday, 08:30–15:00 Saturday and Sunday).

Paleochóra *

Over 20 churches still stand in this atmospheric ghost town that was inhabited between the 9th and 19th century AD when pirate raids forced the islanders to settle inland. The notorious Barbarossa eventually caught up with them in 1538 and ransacked the place.

Paleochóra is located 6.5km (4 miles) east of Aegina Town. In the valley below is **Moní Ágiou Nektários**.

Póros

Just 400m (1312ft) from the mainland, Póros is really two islands separated by a sandy causeway. Many visitors cross to the Peloponnesian town of Galatas which is close to the famous citrus groves of **Lemonodássos**, as well as the ruins of **Troezen** – the legendary birthplace of Theseus. Back on the island, attractive **Póros Town** has a small archaeological museum and views across the narrow straits to the Argolid Mountains. The 18th-century **Monastery of Zoodóchos Pigí**, nestled in pine woods, is just a short bus ride away – or you could venture further to the remains of a Temple of Poseidon (more for the views than the ruins themselves).

Hydra

Seemingly barren and uninviting, Hydra has a surprise in store the moment you slip into the stunning little harbour of Hydra Town. Encircled by tiers of whitewashed houses, this exquisite little port is lined with cafés and shops and bristles with yachts and fishing boats. The island wasn't settled properly until the 15th century. The first inhabitants were shipbuilders and renowned sailors.

Green Tourism

- Take only photographs, leave only footprints.
- Try to use local transport rather than a car.
- Conserve water.
- Buy local products and patronize local restaurants.

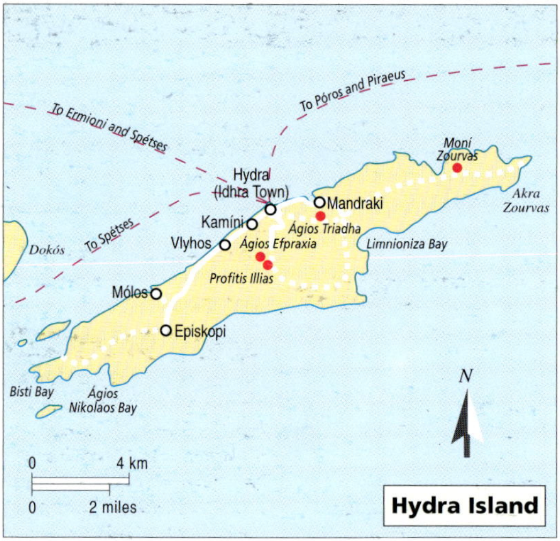

(many of them indulging in a little privateering as the town's 18th-century mansions will attest). Nowadays, Hydra is more renowned for its artists' colony and the doleful-looking donkeys that are the island's main mode of transport. Beaches are not its strong point – the only half-decent one is at Mandraki, a 20-minute walk from town.

Hydra Town ***

Most visitors stay on the waterfront with its wall-to-wall cafés, galleries and jewellery shops – perfect for curio hunting or sipping a *frappé* while watching the donkeys and boats go by. However, a short walk behind this 'tourist façade' leads you into a delightful maze of narrow, winding and often deserted streets – well worth losing yourself in. Back down at the harbour, the **Museum of Hydra** (open 09:00–16:30 Tuesday–Sunday) looks at the island's seafaring contribution to Greek history. There are also some lovely churches, such as the harbourside **Panagía tis Theotókou**.

Sálamis

Largest of the Saronic Gulf islands, Sálamis is the least developed for tourism. Only 1km (0.6 mile) from Piraeus, many people commute by ferry between the island and mainland. Best known as the site of the Battle of Sálamis in 480BC, the island's limited tourist attractions include the fishing harbour and old mansions at Ágios Nikolaos, the 17th-century monastery of Faneromeni and the resort of Peristeria.

Spétses

Lying furthest from Athens, Spétses tends to be quieter and more relaxed than other islands in the Saronic Gulf – despite being featured in John Fowles' *The Magus* and receiving a mini tourism boom in the 1980s as a result.

Covered in pines, the island has some pleasant **beaches**, such as Ágioi Anárgyri and Ágia Paraskeví – both offering water sports. Spétses Town has several **neoclassical mansions** built by wealthy naval merchants and an **old harbour** with shipyards dating from the 17th century.

The Saronic Gulf Islands At a Glance

Best Times To Visit

Summer is very popular, so reserve accommodation well in advance. Mock sea battles are staged in Hydra harbour during the Miaoulia Festival (late June) and at Spétses during the *Armata* (early September).

Getting There

Several companies offer cruises to the islands (*see* page 77). Ferries and hydrofoils make numerous daily voyages between Piraeus and the islands. Ferries leave from the main docks, while most hydrofoils depart from Zéa Marina. Journey times by hydrofoil/ferry to Aegina are 0.5/1.5hr; Póros 1/2.5hr; Hydra 1.25/3.5hr and Spétses 2.5/4.5hr. Schedules are available from the Tourist Information office in Athens. There are daily ferries between the Saronic Gulf Islands.

Getting Around

Aegina: Buses from Aegina Town depart from near the quay to Ágia Marina, the Temple of Aphaia and Nektários Monastery.
Póros: Water taxis make the five-minute crossing from Póros Town to Galatas and various beaches. A bus goes to Moní Zoödohou, while mopeds and bicycles can be hired.
Hydra: Water taxis run from Hydra Town to the island's beaches. Donkeys are available for carrying you and/or your luggage from the waterfront to your hotel.
Spétses: Water taxis link the island to Kosta with onward buses to Nafplio. Horse-drawn carriages can be hired around Spétses Town and there are buses to and from Ág. Marína and Ág. Anárgyri.

Where to Stay

Aegina Town

Luxury
Eginitiko Arhontiko, Thomaïdou, tel: 229 702 4968. Converted 19th-century mansion.
Mid-range
Pavlou, 21 Aeginitou, tel: 229 702 2795. Comfortable, family-run guest house.

Póros

Luxury
Sirene, tel: 229 802 2741. This hotel near the monastery has a pool and private beach.
Mid-range
Seven Brothers, Plateía Iroön, tel: 229 802 3412. A block away from the waterfront with comfortable, air-conditioned rooms.

Hydra Town

Luxury
Orloff, tel: 229 805 2564. Beautiful, 19th-century mansion near the harbour.
Mid-range
Miranda, tel: 229 805 2230. Lovely town house; once the mansion of a sea captain.
Budget
Hydra, tel: 229 805 2102. High on the hill above the harbour; wonderful views.

Spétses Town

Luxury
Possidonion, tel: 229 807 2308. Edwardian-style hotel on the waterfront.
Mid-range
Villa Marina, tel: 229 807 2646. Centrally located, small and friendly.

Where to Eat

The harbour at **Aegina Town** has plenty of restaurants with good seafood tavernas near the fish market. **Póros Town** has a great selection of tavernas. Try Karavolos, Platanos, Caravella and The Flying Dutchman. **Hydra Town** has a plethora of places – try Xeri Elia and To Kryfo Limani. **Spétses'** old harbour has excellent seafood tavernas, including Exedra, Liotrivi and Tarsanas.

Useful Contacts

Port Authority:
Aegina, tel: 229 702 2328; Póros, tel: 229 802 2274; Hydra, tel: 229 805 2279; Spétses, tel: 229 807 2245.
Scuba diving: Hydra Divers, Hydra, tel: 229 805 3900.
Tourist information:
Saitis Tours, Hydra Town, tel: 229 805 2184, produces a guide *Holidays in Hydra*.
Tourist police: Aegina, tel: 229 702 7777; Póros Town, tel: 229 802 2256; Hydra Town, tel: 229 805 2205; Spétses, tel: 229 807 3100.
Walking tours:
Lisa Bartsiokas, Hydra, tel: 229 805 3836.

6
The Peloponnese

Myth meets history on this irresistable peninsula that clings to the Greek mainland by no more than the bridges spanning the **Corinth Canal**. In the minds of ancient Greeks, this 'improbable plane leaf' produced the Hydra, Pegasus, the goddess Demeter and many other mythical creatures ands gods. It was here that Heracles laboured and where the terrible curse of the House of Atreus took its toll. The heart of the Mycenaean empire some 3500 years ago, the Peloponnese is an archaeologist's dream, transforming legend into stone at the awesome site of **Ancient Mycenae**.

Nearby is idyllic **Epidaurus**, an ancient spa that still packs in the crowds at its famous theatre during the annual drama festival of Greek classics. From the well-preserved Roman ruins of **Ancient Corinth** to the Venetian fortress and elegant neoclassical architecture of Greece's old capital, **Nafplio**, the Peloponnese makes a superb excursion from Athens. At a pinch, you could visit the main sites of Argolis in a day trip, but there's so much to see here that you'll probably end up coming back for more.

Over to the west of the Peloponnese is **Ancient Olympia** – quite a trek from Athens, but worth a couple of days exploring its remarkable past as the birthplace of the Olympic Games. Here you will find the ruins of several temples and a wonderful stadium. And if you come this far, why not spend a little time delving into the south of the peninsula – a rugged mosaic of mountains and rocky coasts, dabbed with lush olive and citrus groves.

Don't Miss

*** **Mycenae:** imposing citadel surrounded by Cyclopean walls.
*** **Epidaurus:** superbly-preserved stone theatre.
*** **Nafplio:** atmospheric coastal city; an ideal base from which to explore the region.
*** **Ancient Olympia:** birthplace of the Olympic Games.
** **Ancient Corinth:** remains of a bustling Roman city.
* **Corinth Canal:** historic feat of engineering.

Opposite: *Tall, narrow cypress trees echo the columns of the palaestra at the ruins of Ancient Olympia.*

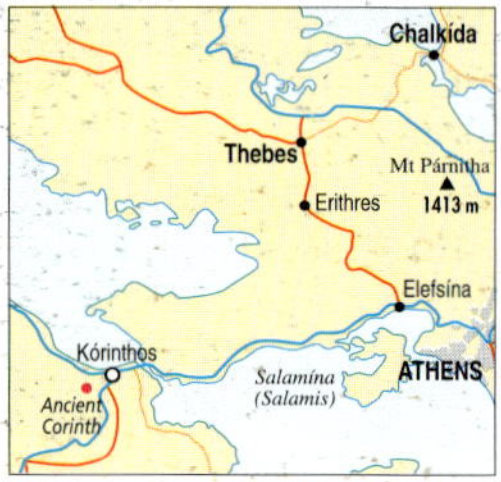

Corinth

Long before **Corinth Canal** (*see* panel, this page) was blasted through the narrow isthmus separating the Saronic and Corinthian gulfs, Corinth was a flourishing centre tapping into the trade route between the eastern Mediterranean and the Adriatic. Athens challenged Corinth's economic dominance in the 5th century BC, but the first big blow came later. Corinthians, with their bawdy and arrogant reputation, apparently sent Roman envoys packing – with excrement on their heads. In hindsight, this was not the smartest move – Romans squashed the city in 146BC. A century later, Caesar rebuilt it and Corinth blossomed again with a population of 750,000. The ruins of Ancient Corinth reveal something of the extent of this major Roman city. Alas, it was destroyed again between the 4th and 6th centuries AD by an undesirable combination of barbarians and earthquakes.

Ancient Corinth **

Well-preserved, the ruins reveal an **agora** (with the **Fountain of Peirene** at its entrance and a capacious **stoa** dating back to the 4th century BC), the **Léchaion Way** (once paved all the way from the city to the port of Lechaion), the **Temple of Octavia** (dedicated to the sister of Emperor Augustus), a 1st-century **odeion** (funded by Hadrian's rich pal, Herodes Atticus) and a **theatre** (tweaked in the 3rd century AD so that water could be piped in for mock sea battles). The most imposing monument is the 550BC **Temple of Apollo**. Seven of the original 38 columns remain standing, each one hewn from single blocks of limestone measuring 7m (24ft) in length. The site's **museum** features 2nd-century Roman floor mosaics and early pottery for which Corinth was famed. Open daily, 08:00–19:00 summer, 08:00–17:00 winter.

Acrocorinth *

Looming above the ruins of Ancient Corinth, this impressive acropolis with its breathtaking views is surrounded by walls some 3km (2 miles) in length. Although many of the fortifications date from medieval times, this prime

Corinth Canal

Started during the reign of Emperor Nero in AD67, the Corinth Canal was not completed until 1893. Measuring 6km (4 miles) in length, the canal is just 23m (75ft) wide. Large modern-day ships are too wide to use this short cut between the Saronic and Corinthian gulfs, but it is still possible to watch smaller cargo vessels and cruise ships slipping past from the vantage of the bridge 90m (295ft) above the water surface.

Above: *The Temple of Apollo at Ancient Corinth.*

spot has changed hands many times and comprises a hotchpotch of different-aged ruins. The first of the imposing **gateways** is Turkish, the second is Frankish and the third is Byzantine – but using plenty of ancient masonry. At the summit are the remains of a **Temple of Aphrodite** where 1000 prostitutes tempted the Corinthians to come up from the city below – much to the indignation of St Paul who duly complained in his 'letters to the Corinthians'.

Argolis

Located on the thumb of the hand-shaped Peloponnese, Argolis contains many archaeological gems. Consider basing yourself in the idyllic historical port of Nafplio for two or three days of relaxed roaming.

Ancient Mycenae ***

The Bronze-Age citadel of Mycenae rears from a rugged melange of mountains and ravines. Even 3300 years after they were built, the city's astounding **Cyclopean walls** leave little to the imagination. In places, they still tower over 12m (39ft) in height. Post-Mycenaean generations, who had lost the ability to move such massive rocks (weighing an average of six tons), believed the giant, Cyclops, must have had a hand in it. Equally impressive is **Lion Gate**. The pair of sculptured (now headless) lions that adorn the main entrance – which leads via a **ramp** to the **palace complex** – are set on a lintel raised 3m (10ft) off the ground and weighing 12 tons. An unsurpassable feat you might think – until, that is, you visit the nearby **Treasury of Atreus** (actually a beehive tomb for a Mycenean king) where the lintel spanning the entrance is no less than 9m (30ft) long and weighs 120 tons.

Ancient Neméa

Three Doric columns mark the site of a 4th century BC temple dedicated to Zeus at this site located roughly halfway between Corinth and Argos, open 08:30–18:00 Tue–Sat. Excavations have also revealed a Hellenistic bathhouse and stadium and a Byzantine village.

Ancient Mycenae stood at the epicentre of the Mycenaean Empire between 1400 and 1100BC. It was at the ruin's treasure-bearing **Grave Circle A**, in 1867, that archaeologist, Heinrich Schliemann, proclaimed, 'I have seen the face of Agamemnon!' – moments before the famous gold death mask crumbled to dust as he lifted it (*see* fact panel on page 68). Open 08:00–19:00 April–September, 08:00–17:00 winter.

LINEAR B

Inscribed on clay tablets found at Mycenae, Tyrins and other ancient sites in the Peloponnese, Linear B script dates from the 14th century BC and was used to record details of commercial transactions and palace administration. Deciphered in 1952 by English architect and scholar, Michael Ventris, this archaic form of writing places the Greek language as the second longest recorded in written history – after Chinese.

Epidaurus ★★★

Snug in a cluster of hills clad in pines and oleanders, the sanctuary of Epidaurus was established around the 6th century BC as a therapeutic centre dedicated to Asklepios, the god of healing. As well as numerous remains, including a **stadium**, **gymnasium**, **stoa**, Doric **temple** and 4th century BC **hotel**, Epidaurus boasts the best preserved **theatre** in Greece. Ideally you should visit early in the day with just one other person who can demonstrate the theatre's near-flawless acoustics by dropping a coin on the stage while you sit 54 rows up in the spectacular scoop of tiered seats.

Nafplio ★★★

Widely regarded as the most elegant city in mainland Greece, Nafplio is a fusion of airy squares and narrow streets with bougainvillea and jasmine spilling from wrought-iron balconies. Allow a day, if you can, to delve into the many **craft shops** and **galleries** and unearth some edible treasures from the numerous **pavement restaurants**.

Below: *The formidable Lion Gate at the entrance to Ancient Mycenae.*

Originally the port of Ancient Mycenae and Argos, Nafplio eventually ended up in Venetian hands in 1388. After a few failed attempts, during which the Venetians built ever stronger defences, including the hill-top **Palamídi Fortress** (open 08:00–19:00 Monday–Friday,

07:30–15:00 Saturday and Sunday) and the picturesque **Boúrtzi** castle lying offshore, the Turks gained control in 1715. Another landmark event in Nafplio's history was its declaration as the capital of Greece from 1828–1834. Three museums worth visiting are the **Folk Art Museum** (open 09:00–14:00 Wednesday–Monday), the **War Museum** (open 09:00–14:00 Tuesday–Sunday) and the **Archaeological Museum** (open 08:30–15:00 Tuesday–Sunday).

The Road to Olympia

Located in the prefecture of Elís, bordering the Ionian coast of the Peloponnese, Ancient Olympia, like Delphi, is a long drive from Athens, but well worth the effort. Inhabited as early as 4000BC, Olympia only achieved esteem as a religious and athletics centre in 776BC when the first Olympic Games were held. A legend describes Heracles marking out the Sanctuary of Olympia and introducing the wild olive – a wreath of which became the Games' traditional crown of victory.

Ancient Olympia ***

Wandering around the relatively compact site, surrounded by wooded hills and rivers, conjures up a vivid sense of the past. You can't help but imagine the roar of a crowd as you walk beneath the archway leading to the **stadium**. Measuring 192m (630ft) in length – equivalent to one *stade* – this extraordinary athletics track still has the indented slabs of the starting line.

Other highlights include the 590BC **Temple of Hera** (originally built of wood in the 8th century BC) and

> **Other Peloponnese Highlights**
>
> **Ancient Messene:** fortified city undergoing excavation on the slopes of Mt Ithómi.
> **Ancient Tiryns:** 13th century BC citadel renowned for its Cyclopean walls of up to 8m (26ft).
> **Mystrá:** spectacular Byzantine ruins perched on a spur of the Taÿgetos range.
> **Monemvasiá:** fortified town built on a rock rising 300m (984ft) above the sea – hence its popular name, the Gibraltar of Greece.
> **Loúsios Gorge:** impressive ravine measuring 5km (3 miles) in length and up to 300m (984ft) deep.

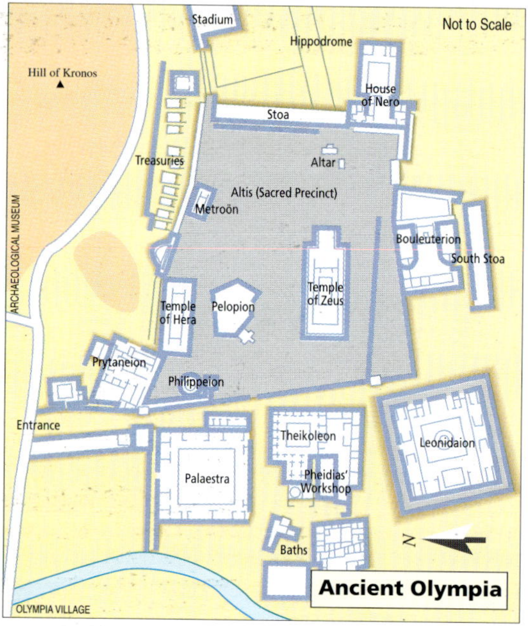

the tumbled columns of the **Temple of Zeus** – a huge Doric temple built in 460BC that housed a majestic enthroned statue of Zeus made from wood, ivory and gold. Regarded as one of the Seven Wonders of the Ancient World, the cult statue was created by the talented Pheidias, whose **workshop** is situated nearby.

Also worth looking out for is the reconstructed colonnade of pillars surrounding the **palaestra**, a training centre for boxers, wrestlers and jumpers. The site is open from 08:00–19:00 daily.

The nearby **Archaeological Museum** (open 12:00–19:00 Monday, 08:00–19:00 Tuesday–Sunday) showcases the many rich finds from Ancient Olympia, such as the pediment and metope sculptures from the Temple of Zeus. The metopes feature the ***Labours of Heracles***, the east pediment shows Pelops and Oenomaos preparing for their chariot race, and the west pediment (finest of all) depicts the ***Battle of Lapiths and Centaurs***. Other important exhibits include a sculptured ***Head of Hera*** (ca.600BC), a painted terracotta of ***Zeus and Ganymede*** from the 5th century BC, and a supremely graceful marble statue of ***Hermes*** – created by Praxiteles around 330BC. The final gallery is devoted to the Olympic Games and contains figurines of athletes, a bronze discus and the remarkable, if perplexing, **Stone of Bybon**. Weighing 143.5kg (316lb), it is inscribed, 'Bybon, son of Phorys, threw me above his head with one hand.' An Olympian feat if ever there was one.

Olympic Legends

According to myth, Zeus won a wrestling contest with Cronus for control of the fertile prefecture of Elís in which Olympia stands and decided to celebrate by founding the first Olympic Games. Another legend describes Heracles marking out the Sanctuary of Olympia and introducing the wild olive – a wreath of which became the Games' traditional crown of victory.

The Peloponnese at a Glance

Best Times To Visit

The Epidaurus Festival takes place in July and August (performances 21:00, Fri and Sat). Classic Greek dramas are staged by the Greek National Theatre. Details from the festival box office, tel: 275 302 2006 or Athens Festival box office, *see* page 76. In July, musical performances take place at the Epidaurus' Mikro Theatro, tel: 210 728 2333.

Getting There

Many companies offer tours to the Peloponnese, *see* page 77.
To Ancient Corinth: Trains (1.75hr) and buses (1.5hr) link Athens and modern Corinth. Corinth bus station (opposite the train station) is near the departure point for buses to Ancient Corinth (5km / 3 miles).
To Ancient Mycenae: Buses from Athens serve Fíchti village, 3km (1.8 miles) from the ancient ruins. Taxis and buses (from Nafplio and Argos) run daily from here to the site.
To Epidaurus: Special buses operate from Athens and Nafplio during the festival. Hydrofoils depart from Piraeus to Palaiá Epidaurus via Aegina.
To Nafplio: Buses (2.5hr) leave hourly from Athens Termnial A.
To Ancient Olympia: Three buses daily from Athens via Pyrgos (5.5hr).

Getting Around

There are frequent buses from Nafplio to Argos (30min) and three times daily to Mycenae (1hr) and Epidaurus (40min). Car hire is available in Nafplio at Auto Europe, 51 Bouboulínas, tel: 275 202 4160.

Where to Stay

Ancient Corinth
Mid-range
Shadow, tel: 274 103 1232. On the northwestern edge of the village surrounding the ruins. Basic, clean rooms.

Mycenae
Mid-range
La Petite Planete, tel: 275 107 6240. Comfortable hotel between the modern village and the ruins.

Budget
Belle Helene, tel: 275 107 6225. Archeologist Heinrich Schliemann stayed in Room 3 of this small hotel which now has a modern resturant.

Nafplio
Luxury
Ilion, 6 Kapodistriou, tel: 275 202 5114. Renovated mansion with lavish facilities.

Mid-range
Byron, 2 Plátanos, tel: 275 202 2351. Beautifully restored building in the old town.

Budget
Dimétris Békas, 26 Efthiopoúlou, tel: 275 202 4594. Well located in old town with a rooftop terrace offering views.

Olympia
Luxury
Europa, tel: 262 402 2650. Modern hotel with hilltop views and excellent facilities.

Mid-range
Pelops, 2 Vareia, tel: 262 402 2543. Small, pleasant family-run hotel.

Budget
Poseidon, 8 Stefanopoulou, tel: 262 402 2576. Good value pension with clean rooms and a popular bar and restaurant.

Where to Eat

Ancient Corinth has limited places to eat, although **Marinos** and **Tassos** are worth seeking out. The modern settlements near the ancient ruins of Mycenae and Olympia tap into the passing coach tour trade with a spattering of restaurants and cafés. In Nafplio there is a line of restaurants along Bouboulínas overlooking the port, plus lots more tucked into the old town and around the squares. The following tavernas are highly recommended: **O Vasílis**, **To Fanária**, and **Zorbás**, all on Staïkopoúlou; **Poseidon** and **Tou Stelára** on Bouboulínas.

Useful Contacts

Tourist information, 25 Martíou, Nafplio, tel: 275 202 4444; Kondilis, Olympia, tel: 262 402 3100.
Tourist police, Nafplio, tel: 275 202 1051.

Travel Tips

Tourist Information

The Greek National Tourist Organisation (**EOT**) is represented in several countries:
UK, 4 Conduit Street, London, W1R 0DJ, tel: 020 7734 5997, fax: 020 7287 1369, www.tourist-offices.org.uk/Greece
USA, Olympic Tower, 645 5th Avenue, New York 10022, tel: 212 421 5777, fax: 212 826 6940, www.greektourism.com
Australia, 51 Pitt Street, Sydney, NSW 2000, tel: 02 9241 1663/4/5, fax: 02 9235 2174.
Canada, 1300 Bay Street, Toronto, Ontario M5R 3K8, tel: 416 968 2220, fax: 416 968 6533.
In **Athens**, the EOT has offices at 2 Amerikis St, Syntagma, tel: 210 331 0561, www.gnto.gr open 09:00–16:00 Mon–Fri, 10:00–15:00 Sat, and at **Elefthérios Venizélos International Airport**, Arrivals Terminal, tel: 210 353 0445, open 08:00–22:00 daily.
The **Tourist Police**, tel: 171 (07:00–23:00 daily), answer (in English) tourist queries and help with emergencies. For local information centres *see* At a Glance for each chapter.

Embassies and Consulates:
Australia, 37 D. Soútsou, Ambelokipi, tel: 210 645 0404, fax: 210 646 6595.
Canada, 4 Ionna Gennadíou, Evangelismos, tel: 210 727 3400, fax: 210 725 3460.
New Zealand, 268 Kifissías, Halandri, tel: 210 687 4701, fax: 210 687 4444.
South Africa, 60 Kifissías, Maroussi, tel: 210 610 6645, fax: 210 610 6636.
UK, 1 Ploutarchou, Kolonáki, tel: 210 727 2600, fax: 210 727 2720.
USA, 91 Vasilissis Sofías, Ambelokipi, tel: 210 721 2951, fax: 210 645 6282.

Entry Requirements

Visitors from EU countries, Australia, Canada, the USA and New Zealand need only a valid passport for entry. Citizens of EU countries can stay indefinitely – but if working, a residence permit must be obtained from the Aliens Bureau, tel: 210 647 6000. Citizens of non-EU countries can stay for up to three months. Apply for extensions at the Aliens Bureau at least 20 days before your initial entry period expires.

Customs

Duty-free restrictions no longer apply within the EU. For non-EU citizens, the duty-free allowance includes 1 litre of spirits or two litres of wine; 200 cigarettes or 50 cigars and 50g of perfume.

Health Requirements

No vaccinations are required for entry into Greece. Emergency medical care is available to EU citizens. All visitors are advised to arrange their own comprehensive travel and medical insurance. Prior to travel, UK residents should complete a Form E111 (available from post offices). In theory, this covers the costs of basic treatment, but in Greece you may still be asked to pay up-front in which case keep the receipts and make a claim back home.

Getting There

By air: International flights arrive at **Elefthérios Venizélos International Airport**, 27km (17 miles) northeast of Athens city centre (*see* Athens At a Glance, page 70). The following airlines have offices in Athens: **Air Canada**,

8 Zirioi St, Maroússi, tel: 210 617 5321; **Air France**, 18 Vouliagménis, Glyfáda, tel: 210 960 1100; **Alitalia**, 577 Vouliagménis, tel: 210 998 8888; **American Airlines**, 15 Panepistimíou, tel: 210 331 1045; **British Airways**, 1 Themistokléos, Glyfáda, tel: 210 890 6666, www.ba.com **KLM**, 41 Vouliagménis, Glyfáda, tel: 210 960 5010; **Lufthansa**, 10 Zirioi, Maroússi, tel: 210 617 5200; **Olympic Airways**, 96 Syngroú, tel: 210 966 6666, www.olympic-airways.gr **Singapore Airlines**, 9 Xenofondos, tel: 210 324 4113; **United Airlines**, 5 Syngroú, tel: 210 924 1389. From the UK, flights operate to Athens with Olympic Airways, British Airways, Virgin Airlines, HelasJet and the no-frills airline, EasyJet, tel: 210 967 0000, www.easyjet.com In summer, Olympic Airways, the national carrier, also flies direct to Athens from New York, Boston, Montreal and Toronto.
By rail: To reach Athens by train from London involves taking Eurostar (tel: 0870 160 6600, www.eurostar.co.uk) to Paris (3 hours) and changing for Brindisi (24 hours). Ferries from Brindisi serve the city of Pátras in the Peloponnese, from where trains operate to Athens. An interesting alternative would be to travel via Venice and board a ferry there.
By road: The best route for **driving** from London to Athens is to take a cross-channel car ferry or the Channel Tunnel (tel: 0870 535 3535, www.eurotunnel.com) across the English Channel before heading south through Reims, Geneva, Milan and on to any of the Italian ferry ports serving Greece (*see* By sea for ferry services). Non-EU citizens require an international driving licence. International **bus** services link various European capitals with Athens, usually via a ferry crossing from Italy. Operators in London include Busabout, tel: 020 7950 1661, www.busabout.com and Eurolines, tel: 0870 514 3219, www.gobycoach.com
By sea: Ferries depart from the Italian ports of Ancona, Bari, Brindisi and Venice. There are daily services from Ancona and Brindisi to Pátras. Crossings take 15–20 hours. From Pátras it is a 220km (137-mile) drive to Athens. Ferry operators include: ANEK Lines, tel: 210 323 3481, and Superfast Ferries, tel: 210 331 3252. Bookings can be made at www.greekferries.gr

What to Pack

Take a comfortable pair of shoes with sturdy grips to cope with the uneven and occasionally slippery marble surfaces at archaeological sites. A sun hat, sunglasses and sunblock are also essential. Evenings, even in summer, can be quite chilly, so remember to pack a lightweight jacket or sweater. A universal plug for a washbasin could also come in useful.

Money Matters

The **euro** (€) replaced the drachma as the currency of Greece in January 2002. Notes are available in 5, 10, 20, 50, 100, 200 and 500 euro denominations, with coins of €1, €2, 50 cents (¢), 20¢, 10¢, 5¢, 2¢ and 1¢. Banks are widespread in Athens (particularly in the Omónia and Syntagma districts). Banking times are 08:20–14:00 Mon–Thu, 08:00–13:30 Fri. Travellers cheques are widely accepted (take your passport as proof of ID when cashing them) and there are numerous 24-hour cash dispensers (ATMs). Credit cards are accepted in most hotels, car rentals and travel agencies, major shops and restaurants. Small hotels, gift shops and tavernas, however, may only take cash.

Accommodation

Athens offers an excellent range of accommodation. **Hotels** in Greece are classified in six categories: Luxury, A, B, C, D and E. Generally, luxury hotels cost upwards of €100 for a double room per night, while D and E category hotels charge up to around €40.

National Holidays

1 January • New Year's Day
6 January • Epiphany
February or March • Shrove Monday (41 days before Easter)
25 March • Independence Day
March or April • Good Friday, Easter Monday
1 May • Labour Day
May or June • Whit Monday (50 days after Easter)
15 August • Feast of the Assumption
28 October • *Óchi* Day
25 December • Christmas Day

Prices are often discounted during the winter low season. Reservations are imperative during the high season (July–August). For accommodation visit www.greekhotel.com
Camping (around ¤5 per night) is a good budget option in rural areas. Only use authorized campsites; see www.greecetravel.com/campsites
Self-catering apartments and villas can be booked through travel agents – although most focus on the Greek islands.

Eating Out

Athens caters for locals eating Greek food at Greek times, as well as tourists seeking familiar food at familiar times. If you want to go Greek, take a light breakfast of yoghurt and honey followed by a mid-morning snack (a cheese pie or sesame seed bread ring). Lunch is late (starting around 14:00) and can be a lengthy, social affair with wine. Then it's time for the all-important siesta followed by an evening drink and a late dinner at about 22:00. Expect to pay around ¤10 per person for a typical taverna meal with wine.

Transport

Greece has a comprehensive public transport system. Getting around in Athens or exploring further afield is cheap and straightforward.
Air: Olympic Airways (*see* Getting There, page 123) operates most domestic flights. Baggage allowance is 15kg (33lb). Popular destinations from Athens include Santorini, Mikonos, Rhodes, Crete, Thessaloníki, and around 30 other islands and mainland cities. Most flights take 50–60 minutes. Airport tax of €12 is included in the price for domestic flights.
Rail: The Greek Railway Organisation (OSE) is gradually updating its rolling stock, although train travel can still be painfully slow. It is, however, incredibly cheap, with the 5-hour route from Athens–Pátras costing around ¤8 first class. Schedules and fares can be found at www.ose.gr or tel: 210 529 7777. The metro (*see* Athens At a Glance, page 71) is the best way to travel across the capital, with three main lines providing access to most major sites, as well as locations in Greater Athens, such as Piraeus and Kifissiá.
Bus: The regional bus service (KTEL, www.ktel.org) operates a comprehensive network of efficient services between all main centres. *See* Athens At a Glance, page 72 for a list of terminals and destinations. In Athens, blue and white **suburban buses** and overhead cable **trolley buses** operate from 05:00–24:00. A map showing routes can be obtained from the EOT (*see* Tourist Information, page 122), while tickets can be purchased from transport kiosks or news stands (*periptera*).
Car: Driving in Athens is not for the faint-hearted. Preserve your sanity by travelling to the city's sites using the metro, buses, taxis or by walking. If you need independence for exploring further afield, consider taking a bus to the international airport and collecting a **rental car** from there. The following companies have offices in the city and at the airport: **Avis**, 48 Amalias, tel: 210 322 4951 or 210 353 0578; **National**, 58-60 Spiroupatsi, tel: 210 346 3588 or 210 353 3323; **Europcar**, 4 Syngrou, tel: 210 924 8810 or 210 353 0580; **Hertz**, 12 Syngrou, tel: 210 922 0102 or 210 353 4900; **Sixt**, 23 Syngrou, tel: 210 922 0171 or 210 353 0576. The minimum driving age is 18 years. Speed limits are 50kph (30mph) in built-up areas, 120kph (75mph) on highways and 90kph (60mph) on other roads. Seat belts must be worn and there are heavy penalties for driving under the influence of alcohol. Road distances from Athens to Corinth, Nafplio, Pátras and Thessaloníki are 84km (52 miles), 165km (102 miles), 220km (137 miles) and 513km (319 miles) respectively.
Ferry: The two main hubs for ferry transport throughout Greece are Piraeus and Rafína. Information is available at www.greekferries.gr Hydrofoils are generally twice as fast as ferries – but cost about twice as much.

DRIVING

EXIT • *éxothos*
ENTRANCE • *ísothos*
SLOW • *argá*
NO PARKING • *apagorévete ee státhmevsis*
Where is the road to…? • *Poo íne o thrómos yía…?*
Where can I buy petrol? • *Poo boró n'agorásso venzini?*

Travel Passes: Daily 24-hour travel passes for around ¤3 are available for use on Athens buses, trolley buses and metro. **Organized Tours:** Several tour operators in Athens offer excursions to highlights within the city and beyond to the Peloponnese, Saronic Islands, Cape Sounion and Delphi, *see* Athens at a Glance, page 77.

Business Hours

Shops are generally open 09:00–15:00 Mon and Wed, 09:00–19:00 Tue, Thu and Fri, 08:30–15:30 Sat, closed Sun. Tourist shops and department stores often stay open longer. For opening times of **archaeological sites** and **museums**, refer to individual attractions. Normal hours are 08:00 or 09:00 to 14:00 or 15:00 Tue–Sun, closed Mon. **Churches** and **monasteries** often close for a few hours during the middle of the day. **Banks** open 08:20–14:00 Mon–Thu, 08:00–13:30 Fri, while **kiosks** (*periptera*) are open early until late.

Time Differences

Athens is Greenwich Mean Time (GMT) +2, Central European Time +1 and North American Eastern Standard Time +7. Clocks go forward an hour from last Sunday in March to last Sunday in October.

Communications

Post offices (*tachidromío*) are easily identified by bright yellow signs. In Athens, the main ones are at Syntagma Square and 100 Eolou, Omónia, open 07:30–20:00 Mon–Fri, 07:30–14:00 Sat, 09:00–13:00 Sun. Stamps (*grammatósima*) are also sold at kiosks and tourist shops (but often with a 10% surcharge). Postcards and letters take up to seven days to reach the UK and 11 days to Australia and the USA. Express service ensures three-day delivery within the EU. Phone cards (*télekartas*) can be purchased at kiosks for use in public **telephones** which allow local and international calls. Press the 'I' (information) button for user instructions in English. To **phone abroad from Greece**, dial 00, followed by the country code, then the city or area code (without the 0 before it) and then the number. To **phone Greece from abroad**, dial the country code 30, then the full 10-digit number. In Athens, standard numbers begin with 2, mobile numbers with 6. Send **telegrams** and **faxes** from post offices. Greece has 3 **mobile phone** service providers – CosmOTE, Panafon and Telstet. Rent mobiles from www.greecetravel.com/phones **Internet** and **email** can be accessed from some hotels and several internet cafés in Athens, *see* page 78.

Useful Phrases

Good morning • *Kaliméra*
Good evening • *Kalispéra*
Hello • *Yásas*
Goodbye • *Andío*
Please • *Parakaó*
Thank you • *Evcharistó*
No • *Óchi*
Yes • *Né*
How are you? • *Ti kánete?*
Where is...? • *Poo íne...?*
How much? • *Póso káni?*
What is that? • *Ti íne aftó?*
Do you speak English? • *Milate Anglika?*
I don't understand • *Then katalavéno*

Electricity

The current in Greece is 220V, 50Hz. Plugs are continental two-pin. Buy adapters at electrical stores or large airports.

Weights and Measures

Greece uses the metric system. Commas indicate decimals, while points are used for thousands. Liquids are often sold by weight rather than volume.

Health Precautions

Bottled water is widely available, but Athens' tap water is

Conversion Chart

From	To	Multiply By
Millimetres	Inches	0.0394
Metres	Yards	1.0936
Metres	Feet	3.281
Kilometres	Miles	0.6214
Square kilometres	Square miles	0.386
Hectares	Acres	2.471
Litres	Pints	1.760
Kilograms	Pounds	2.205
Tonnes	Tons	0.984

To convert Celsius to Fahrenheit: x 9 ÷ 5 + 32

safe to drink. In summer, drink plenty of fluids to avoid dehydration and heat exhaustion. Do not underestimate the severity of the sun in Greece. Protect yourself from sunburn by wearing a hat and applying a high factor sunscreen. Also be wary of the black-spined sea urchins along stretches of rocky coast.

Personal Safety

Athens is a safe city. Take normal precautions – leave your passport, tickets and valuables in a hotel safe and carry small amounts of cash and a credit card in a money belt. Be especially vigilant of pickpockets on the metro and at flea markets. Like any large city there are places to be wary of travelling alone at night. If in doubt, seek local advice or stick to popular tourist areas like Pláka. Be wary of 'scam artists' – usually effusively friendly men approaching you in the street or in bars, offering to buy you a drink.

Emergencies

Police tel: 100; **ambulance** tel: 166; **fire brigade** tel: 199. For **emergency hospitals**, tel: 106. **SOS-Doctors**, tel: 1016, is a 24-hour service that charges a fixed rate for hotel visits. Most **pharmacies** are open normal business hours, and a list of after-hours duty pharmacies is published in *Athens News*. The international airport has a permanent 24-hour pharmacy.

Etiquette

A polite greeting – *kalimera* (good day) or *kalispera* (good evening) – always goes down well. In Greece personal questions are not considered rude. Greeks also believe in the evil eye (bad luck as a result of someone's envy), so if, for example, you compliment the beauty of a child, remember to ward off evil spirits by making a ritual 'spitting' sound afterwards. Dress respectfully inside churches and monasteries (covered arms, long trousers or skirts below knees) and make a small donation or buy a candle. Use water sparingly and resist any temptation to pocket bits of carving from ancient sites.

Special Needs

Despite an ongoing programme of facilities for the **mobility impaired**, Athens can be a challenge for wheelchair users. Most major museums and hotels are wheelchair-friendly, but restaurants (often with downstairs toilets) and archaeological sites (with uneven surfaces) can be difficult. The international airport has excellent provision for disabled travellers, while the metro system (with lifts to the platforms) and the growing number of pedestrianized streets make things easier.

Tipping

Although service charge is included in restaurant bills, it is customary (but not obligatory) to leave a small tip of around 10–15%. Taxi drivers, porters and cloakroom attendants will also appreciate a small gratuity of loose change.

Language

Tour guides speak English, French, German and other European languages. Most museums and sites have some interpretation (leaflets, signage, etc.) in English. Greeks appreciate any attempt you make to speak a few words of their language, *see* fact panel, page 125. If you're serious, consider enrolling at a language school in Athens. Contact the tourist office for details.

Good Reading

- **Andrewes, Antony** (1967) *Greek Society*, Penguin. Description of society in ancient Greece.
- **Graves, Robert** (1955) *The Greek Myths*, Penguin. Adventures of the main gods and heroes.
- **Kazantzakis, Nikos** (1995) *The Last Temptation*, Faber & Faber.
- **Kazantzakis, Nikos** (1997) *Zorba the Greek*, Faber & Faber.
- **Meier, Christia** (2000) *Athens: A portrait of the City in its Golden Age*, Pimlico. Detailed insight in to the city's heyday.
- **Miller, Henry** (1975) *The Colossus of Maroussi*, WW Norton. Account of Greece at the outbreak of WWII.
- **Pausanias** *Guide to Greece* (many editions), Penguin. The original travel guide to Greece.
- **Rodley, Lyn** (1996) *Byzantine Art and Architecture: an Introduction*, Cambridge University Press.
- **Woodhouse, CM** (1992) *Modern Greece: A Short History*, Faber & Faber.

INDEX

Note: Numbers in **bold** indicate photographs